WHAT PEOPLE ARE SAYING ABOUT

BREAD NOT STONES

Una Kroll has written a rema̶̶̶̶̶̶̶̶̶̶̶̶̶̶̶̶̶̶̶ ̶rspective both as a medical doctor and as ̶̶̶̶̶̶̶̶̶ ̶women priests in the Church of England. The storie̶ ̶̶̶̶ ̶̶counts reveal a woman with a passionate humanity, brilliant intellect and deep spiritual insight. As both doctor and priest, Una has been a pioneering advocate for women: whether introducing new healthcare treatments or being one of the most outspoken campaigners for women's ordination. Ultimately, though, Una has written a spiritual biography of women's struggle for full inclusion in the Church's ministries and mission, with her most profound reflections revealing an evolving understanding of God as creative energy and unconditional love.

Christina Rees, broadcaster and writer, and member of General Synod of the Church of England.

This is an important book. It documents the life journey of a woman who – as a medical doctor, a missionary nun in Africa, a pioneer of gender equality, a priest in the Church of England, a contemplative Catholic – influenced the lives of thousands of people. She records her own inner struggles of search, doubt, loss of faith and rediscovering God with disarming frankness and deep insight. She narrates the complex stories of individuals she served with great sensitivity and an intense human involvement. We see God in action: as Creative Energy and Unconditional Love. I recommend this book to Christian women who want to know 'from the inside' what early women in ministry had to endure. I recommend the book to those who, like Una Kroll herself, comb the fabric of our modern world in pursuit of an elusive God. I recommend the book to everyone fascinated by the spiritual adventures and practical wisdom of an exceptional champion of a God who is Love.

Dr John Wijngaards, author of *The Ordination of Women in the Catholic Church: Unmasking A Cuckoo's Egg Tradition*

Una Kroll's spiritual journey is unique – a doctor, medical missionary, a nun, a priest, a mother, author, a solitary and spiritual friend of many; this book tells the story of her life with honesty, integrity, sorrow, joy and the loving compassion that makes Una one of the most amazing people I have ever met.

Rt Rev Dominic Walker OGS, former bishop of Monmouth and member of the Oratory of the Good Shepherd

Una's life is driven by her longing to do what she feels God requires of her. She is a mother and grandmother. She is a Doctor but also she has been an anchorite, and a nun living in a religious community. She has stood on the platform of Women's Rights for Parliament. She is a well-known author and commentator on matters religious. This book is a page turner.

Donald Reeves MBE, Anglican priest, former rector of St James Piccadilly; Director of the Soul of Europe

Una Kroll: Mystic, Physician, Feminist, Rebel, Priest-Theologian, Activist and Contemplative Nun, at the heart of life yet never far from the edge. Like real life, her pilgrimage is full of contradictions, astonishing, outrageous, and despite herself, authentically Christian. An adventurous read.

Paul Oestreicher, Anglican Priest and Quaker, former director of Coventry Cathedral's Centre for International Reconciliation.

Una Kroll has written her interesting autobiography with an openness and clarity that manages to explore deep theological truths and complex experiences in a way that is understandible, engaging and encourages useful reflection. She uses her own experiences, and those of others, to explore the changes of direction in her work and life as wife, mother, doctor and priest and explain candidly where she is now. This is, she says, as she approaches the end of her life. Of particular interest to me was how she transformed past wounds into a creative present, particularly her experience as a campaigner for women's ministry in the Anglican Church, and justice in institutional Christianity. Now she has discovered an understanding and partnership with those with whom she disagrees. Her writing about Unconditional Creative Love is inspirational and illustrates convincingly how transformation happens and now she can work with, and understand, those opposed to her views, if their work is "pointing to love." This is helpful for those engaged in prophetic and potentially confrontational work in campaigning groups such as Catholic Women's Ordination (CWO) of which she and I are both members. (CWO campaigns for women's ordained ministry in a renewed Catholic Church.) Her book helps to explain how one can, with integrity, become or remain a Catholic, willingly nourished by its sacramental radical vision of love, some of its social teaching and contemplative tradition, yet seeing its institutional flaws and wishing to reform what has increasingly become more of an unresponsive, clerical, patriarchical institution. I used to listen to Una on the radio in the 1970s and came to recognise she had planted a seed which remained dormant in my own life until the 1990s. I knew she had recently become a Catholic and this book helped me, and will explain to others, why she took this step to jump "from the frying pan into the fire" for a woman seeking institutional justice for women, first in the Anglican and now the Catholic Church.

Pippa Bonner, CWO (Catholic Women's Ordination)

Bread Not Stones:

the Autobiography of an Eventful Life

Bread Not Stones:

the Autobiography of an Eventful Life

Una Kroll

CHRISTIAN
ALTERNATIVE

Winchester, UK
Washington, USA

First published by Christian Alternative Books, 2014
Christian Alternative Books is an imprint of John Hunt Publishing Ltd.,
Laurel House, Station Approach,
Alresford, Hants, SO24 9JH, UK
office1@jhpbooks.net
www.johnhuntpublishing.com
www.christian-alternative.com

For distributor details and how to order please visit the 'Ordering' section on our website.

Text copyright: Una Kroll 2014

ISBN: 978 1 78279 804 0

A CIP catalogue record for this book is available from the British Library.

Design: Stuart Davies

Printed and bound by CPI Group (UK) Ltd, Croydon, CR0 4YY

We operate a distinctive and ethical publishing philosophy in all
areas of our business, from our global network of authors to
production and worldwide distribution.

CONTENTS

For Helen Dacey my friend, and for my ten grandchildren:
Alex, Simon, David, Joshua, Lilly, Rona, Liam, Nick, Maisha
and Vivian.

Introduction

I am a person whose life has been influenced by a 'mysterious force' that I have never fully understood since it first made itself known to me in 1930 when I was a very young child on a train journey to Latvia with my mother. The 'force', a kind of warm energy without form, shape, identity, or name, felt real to me; though I could not describe it then, nor can I now. The warm sense of peace did not stay with me very long, but a couple of years later, when I was in Riga away from my mother and very unhappy, the same feeling reappeared through my Auntie Nellie who was living in the same town at that time. Later, when I had returned home, 'it' made itself present to me near a dim white light in a dark church in Finsbury Park, London. By that time I had heard about God so, from the age of seven, I identified this 'mysterious energy' as God, but I did not think of God as a person. Jesus Christ was a storybook character, a heroic figure rather like the heroes and heroines of all the other fairy tales and mythological characters that fed my developing imagination and enthusiasms.

In 1944, when I was nineteen years old, I encountered this 'mysterious force' again during a vigorous argument about Jesus when I was a medical student at Cambridge University in England. I did not understand what had happened so I went to an Anglican priest for help. It was he who told me that Christ was not a fairy tale, but God. Subsequently, I received some 'proper' instruction from this priest who turned out to be an Anglican Franciscan friar. As a result of our relationship I became an enthusiastic Anglo-Catholic Christian.

In 1953, after several years of a rather ascetic lifestyle in the tradition I had embraced, I lapsed from the rules of my Church by committing adultery. I did not lose my faith but, by throwing off the chains of my strict moral upbringing, I realised that I had banished myself from the 'club'. And as a sign of my liberation from conventional Christian morality I had my ears pierced and bought some gold earrings: then a rather daring gesture for a 'nicely' brought up person to make. By this time I was an ambitious young doctor who wanted to become a neurosurgeon. I was also determined to remain a sexually liberated woman who would necessarily forgo having children. At the time I thought it would have been difficult for a woman of my particular generation to combine a professional career with marriage and motherhood.

Nine months later, in December 1953, again at the behest of this 'mysterious force' that had caused me to act impetuously at the time of my original conversion, I took my earrings out and decided to become an Anglican medical missionary nun. Even now I do not think this was a mistake for it did lead to new paths which I describe in this book. This 'mysterious force' that I did not understand – but that, rightly or wrongly, I named as God, Father, Son and Holy Spirit – took me to Liberia in West Africa in 1956, after I was professed in simple vows in the Anglican Community of the Holy Name. In 1957, while I was in their mission station in Liberia trying to combine the life of a nun with that of a doctor, I realised that I was not suited to this double life.

I left my Order in disgrace because I married an ex-monk, who had been in life vows in an American Order that also worked in Liberia. Yes, we knew we had betrayed our vows: yes, we were penitent, but knew we could not return to our Communities. We sought reconciliation from the Anglican Churches in America and England. We then accepted our joint punishment, and Leo was unable to act as a priest for many years. I had destroyed any chance of a career in neurosurgery, or in any medical speciality. We were out on our own. I could still be a general medical practitioner. But Leo took a variety of secular jobs for the rest of his life, because he was 'blacklisted' by the Archbishop of Canterbury and so was unable to get paid employment in the Anglican Church.

It is not a very unusual story, either in the Anglican Church or in the Catholic Church. Two people long to serve God as celibates, but find they cannot do so. The various adventures of our married years are documented in this book. They demonstrate what many sinners know very well. Neither sin, nor wrongdoing in the eyes of the institutional guardians of morality, can destroy faith, nor can it quench a sincere desire to serve God as dedicated Christians. It is true that sometimes Christian sinners do abandon their faith, but in our own case the journey through the restorative justice and mercy of that 'mysterious force', that we called God, was for both of us, a journey towards the freedom of love and healing during the thirty years of our marriage.

In 1987, then aged sixty-one, I was widowed. My journey had to continue alone. A year later I returned to being a novice in a different religious community, as a nun in simple vows. Finally, I left community life altogether to become a 'solitary' in life vows. And I have lived like that since then. But in 1997, at the age of seventy-one, past the normal retiring age for clergy of that denomination, I was ordained to the priesthood of the Church in Wales. That felt like purgatory for, at that time, I *felt* that I had lost my faith; yet I continued to practice as an Anglican and as a priest of the Church in Wales. I had yet more to learn from that 'mysterious force' that I could no longer name, feel to be present, or describe; yet who, I now believe, continued to draw me into new ways of living my life.

My journey continued after I retired to England in 2003, and forms the majority of my account in Chapters Six and Seven. It continues in 2014, and I recount this part of the story in the last two chapters of this book. I want to share it with people who have sinned, made mistakes, been punished by Church or State, and with those who have managed to live upright, God-fearing lives all their lives. The truths that I am trying to tell in writing this book are that all human beings are capable of sin, of making mistakes that cannot be put right, and of wounding God. Yet God continues to love us, and if we let God go on loving us, our lives *will* be changed by that compassionate love *and* bring us into a new and vibrant love: because God has travelled with us. That for me is what I celebrate as I near the end of my life; an eventful life, yes, but a parable of God's love for everyone and everything in creation.

During my journey through this unconventional life I have been brought into contact with a number of people who have also met with this 'mysterious force' that has brought about changes in lifestyle that have had profound effects on the course of their lives. Some of the stories in this book are about the interweaving of our lives. They show that despite grave sin, despite mistaken choices, despite our wounds, we can still become people who, because we are loved by God, can be used by God in all sorts of ways, both inside and outside the walls of the institutional Churches.

Chapter 1

Beginnings

I started my life of religious faith, without knowing it, in 1926 when I was baptised as an infant into the Church of England. My parents and my godparents made that choice on my behalf, perhaps without much understanding of what they were doing. It was a cultural norm at the time, one for which I am grateful.

My mother, Hilda Evelyn Pediani, had been raised in Russia. Her mother, Victoria, was the daughter of Octavius Temple, one of the brothers of the Archbishop of Canterbury, Dr Frederick Temple (1). European families were great colonisers at that time so she accompanied her father to Constantinople where he practised medicine. My English grandmother and Italian grandfather met in Constantinople and they eloped. Victoria was denounced and cut off from her family. She and her Italian Catholic husband went to live in St Petersburg. They had seven children, all initially baptised as Catholics, but then secretly taken by my Anglican grandmother to an Anglican chaplain and re-baptised as Anglicans. My mother was the youngest child of their family. Her father, an Italian tobacco merchant, was convinced that her destiny lay in marriage and motherhood, so he educated her for that role. Hilda became a skilled linguist, an above average pianist, a competent seamstress and an attractive young woman. She was not expected to earn her own living.

My father, George Alexander Hill, (1892-1968) was the eldest son of an emigrant British timber merchant. Born in Estonia, he, his sister and brother, were brought up in Russia among the group of merchants who lived there. He was fluent in many languages. When the First World War broke out in 1914 he promptly joined the Canadian army, fought at Ypres and was seriously wounded. He then joined the British Intelligence. The

First World War brought an end to my mother and father's former way of life. They were both intelligence agents for the British government and their lives became intertwined in those roles. Although my father was already married, they did not marry then. But in 1918 they escaped from Russia and came to Britain. The rest of their families scattered to live in different European countries. My father remained in intelligence work (2). He and his first wife had two daughters. In 1925 he left them to marry my pregnant mother so that I, conceived in Rome, would not become a bastard child. The moral climate of the time demanded that solution among my father's family.

When I was eighteen months old my father disappeared from our lives to return to a former lover whom he subsequently married. My mother and I lived in England in poverty. My mother was unhappy. Her sorrow at her husband's absence from our lives expressed itself in hatred for him, the person whom she blamed for our plight. Her vigorous love and vigorous hatred spurred us into survival. Love and hatred were transferred on to my mother's moral attitudes towards my 'good' and 'bad' behaviour as she brought me up according to the strict moral climate of the time. My mother had not been educated for any profession so she made our living by working in a basement 'sweat shop' with some friends who were Russian exiles, making and selling clothes. My father's sister, Marguerite, a British Army wife whose husband later joined the Royal Air Force, bailed us out from time to time.

Our poverty was related to my mother's lack of formal education so she fought to educate me in the best possible way. My childhood was turbulent in that, although we were based in London, we travelled to many European countries to visit relatives and friends. It was during one of my first travels that I first met the 'mysterious force' that I referred to in the introduction to this book.

Two early journeys through painful events

I cannot have been more than three or four years old when I accompanied my mother on my first remembered journey to Latvia, where my grandmother, her daughter Mabel, her German-born husband and their three sons lived. It was a journey I remember vividly, but not the reason for our leaving London. I know it was winter for it was very cold. I remember that we sat on hard wooden seats in a tightly packed third-class carriage. We had some pre-packed food and water with us. So did our companions. At meal times we shared our food with one another. It was sweaty and smelly in that carriage. At night we slept sitting up. At each frontier, passport-control men came and woke us up, looked through our travel documents and slammed the carriage doors shut again. The snores, grunts and fragments of dream speech resumed, until I too fell asleep.

In the morning I was allowed to climb on to the carriage table – no more than a ledge really – to look out of the window. It must have been very early. Behind the mist there was a huge red sun that lit up a dark forest. As I sat there I became aware of an intense pain nearby. It was coming from my mother. When I looked at her tears were running down her face. There was no sound coming from her. When I cried I made a noise. I had never seen her cry. I had never felt such agony in my own body.

Her pain engulfed me. I could not bear to look at her any more. Instead, I looked out of the window. It was then that I experienced my first touch of something that I have experienced many times since. It was as if the pain was suffocating me so strongly that I could not breathe. At the same moment – at exactly the same moment – I was being absorbed by something I could not see or understand that was coming through the window towards me. Dark tall pine trees, flecked with snow, sped past. There was no one there, yet in that instant my pain melted into a sense of joyful peace. Suddenly, I was very hungry. An old lady offered me a boiled sweet. I kept it in my mouth without sucking it. It lasted a long time. My mother did not speak all that day, but I was no longer distressed.

A second story from my later childhood

Those who read this narrative of a young child's memories may say that I am reading into their meaning through adult 'rose coloured' spectacles. All I know is that the experience returned to me some three years later when I spent a year away from my mother in Latvia. The year before this happened my mother had gone through a period of prolonged ill health and could not work. We were living in considerable hardship at this time. Then my mother received an invitation for me to go abroad as a companion to another 'only child', the daughter of one of her friends on overseas service. She sent me. It was not the success she had hoped for. I was miserably homesick – and it showed.

I cried a good deal. I was reprimanded and was then physically punished. I stopped crying. Then I remembered that my Aunt Marguerite, who had accompanied me to the ship on which we sailed, told me that I could send home a coded message if I was really unhappy, by drawing a ship in my letters home. So I drew ship after ship in my letters in the hope that my mother would see the pain that lay behind the picture. But the message I got back was: "How well you draw! Be a good girl. We'll be together again next year." Unfortunately my aunt had forgotten to pass on the code to my mother and I knew nothing of this lapse of memory during that year away from my home country.

After a while, I reached a point of desperation. I had no way of contacting my mother. I felt trapped. I wanted her to come and rescue me, yet somehow I knew that she would not do so. One night, I woke. The room was dark. Night lights, or open doors to a landing light, were not allowed in that house. Reading in bed was forbidden. Dolls and teddy bears were not encouraged. Despair engulfed me. I felt physically crushed, squashed, beaten into pulp. Simultaneously, or so it now seems to my adult memory, something akin to stubborn courage entered my life in the shape of a feeling that was indescribable but comparable to what had happened to me in the Polish forest three years before.

I fell asleep. In the morning I had found a measure of endurance that lasted until my return home some months later. My Auntie Nellie, who was companion to a friend from the Italian embassy in Riga, came to my rescue by suggesting I go to a classical Russian ballet school. It was a lifeline, a recurrent source of joy and hope. I danced with my flickering hope. I was well taught and continued to dance for several years after my return home until my mother decided that ballet had to give way to intellectual learning when I was twelve years old. I mourned my loss, but complied. With hindsight I know she was wise, but I missed the elegance of dance and have never forgotten my pink ballet shoes. A dear artist friend, Rahel Rayner, recently painted two ballet shoes for me as if they were waiting for me to step into them and my eighty-eight-year-old eyes overflowed with tears of joy and pain.

My eighty-eight-year-old reflection on these events

The experiences I have described may happen when people encounter an event in life that could be described as 'dislocating'. It does not kill them, but it does bring them to a 'full stop'. I once received a card from a friend, Donald Nicholl (3), who acted as my work mentor. He sent me a postcard, saying: "I have hit the buffers, Una." Those were the only words on the card. I had to decode them. Knowing him well, I did. He was talking about train buffers, using them as an analogy. Train buffers are sprung to soften impact. They may prevent utter catastrophe, yet, even if the train is travelling slowly the damage may be so great that the engine cannot even reverse. It may have to be 'written off' as unsafe for further service and subsequent examination may reveal a design fault that makes it imperative to construct a new type of engine that is 'fit for purpose'. My friend was telling me that he had come to a 'full stop'. He felt he had run into a buffer. The blow had not killed him, but it had seriously injured him.

While this is no more than an analogy, it depicts the situation of those who have come to the end of their resources, their trust in themselves, in other people, or their faith in God. It may also describe those who have come to the end of hope, those who have terminal illnesses, or who are facing, or living through, bereavement. The analogy may even be of help to those who come to the end of love for a talent, a work, a person, an institution that they have once loved with passion, but for which they no longer feel anything but numb boredom instead of delight.

These 'full stops' in life are so devastating that people sometimes say that they feel as if something inside them has 'died'. They are compelled to go on living, but life is never the same as it was before it happened. Attempts to 'recover faith, hope, or love' fail: as do attempts to 'forget the past' and 'move on'. There seems to be no way out.

Some of the men and women who 'hit the buffers' in the way that I have described, wither away as a result of their injuries. They become hollow. And this hollow space, like a vacuum, may suck in bitterness. Sometimes that bitterness is more visible to others than to themselves. If, however, there is a tiny flame of faith or hope or love in them, it may yet be kindled into a new, although different, kind of life.

It seems to be a feature of many people's adult memory that painful events make more impact than ecstatic ones. Sometimes they plague people when they are adults and hamper their relationships. This is probably why I have written about negative experiences first. The two early events in my own life I have described made a permanent mark on my own life. The first taught me that pain could not destroy my ability to find joy at the same time. The second gave me courage to endure what had to be endured without losing hope that change was ultimately possible. In my own case hope did not disappoint, though its fulfilment took a long time and a great deal of hard work by many people. These events are examples of how negative experience can be transformed in an instant by a counteracting positive feeling. In my adult life as a doctor of medicine and a counsellor I have met others who have had similar experiences.

But a book that dwells only on the transformative changes that can come out of profoundly negative experiences would be incomplete. Positive experiences of great joy can also bring about profound changes in direction. These transformative positive experiences are just as real as the ones that come out of darkness and despair and they are every bit as powerful in achieving life changes as the negative ones.

The following two stories are about occasions, akin to ecstasy, of moments of knowing that I was loved. These come from a little later in my childhood, because that was when I first recognised how wonderful it was to be loved by someone else.

The effects of ecstasy during my childhood

During my childhood years there were several times when I felt deeply happy; so happy that I recognised a change in myself that was akin to the changes that had come into my life out of despair. These moments of joy were, I now know, experiences of the kind that make you feel that all is well with your life and with those with whom you live, and, indeed, with the whole world. They were moments of feeling united with all creation.

One such moment came to me shortly after the events I have already described as painful. It happened on our next visit to Latvia after my mother and I had been reunited when I was seven years old. It was when we went to Latvia for Christmas that I knew the bliss of being loved.

We arrived in the little wooden house at Libau, close to the Baltic Sea. Snow was on the ground. My mother was tired out. Her elder sister, my Auntie Nellie, who was then staying with my Auntie Mabel, her eldest sister, greeted us with warmth. The 'dacha' was warmed by a central iron wood-burning stove. My auntie bundled my mother off to bed. "The youngster can sleep with me," she said.

Sleeping with Auntie Nellie in her high feather bed was an adventure as she habitually slept with her cat inside the bed clothes at her feet. The wooden house was freezing at night times: bed was the warmest place for animals and humans. Auntie Nellie was a large lady with a heart of love and a great sense of fun. Early morning talks, and cups of hot tea from the samovar, strengthened our bonds of affection. That Christmas holiday gave me my first experience of being loved in a way that my then sick, worried and unhappy mother could not give me at the time. It was wonderful.

A little while later I experienced the same feeling of unconditional love in an empty church, lit only by a small twinkling sanctuary light. God, I thought that day, was just like my Auntie Nellie. It was not until many years later that I was told that she was a firm atheist.

When my mother had recovered from her illness and I returned home to England I was a disturbed child. I was angry with my mother and took revenge on her through my bad behaviour. When I was seven years old we moved again, this time to Paris. We lived there for several months because my mother wanted to marry a stateless Russian exile, Nicholas Saveloff. Had they done so, I would have lost my British nationality and become stateless so they decided not to live together then. They eventually married after I grew up. My mother and I returned to England.

A second experience of ecstasy happened when I was about nine years old and our lives had taken a turn for the better.

My mother and I were living in a large 'bed-sitter room' flat in London. I was lying in bed one evening and my mother was across the room with her needlework in her hands. She was a skilled seamstress: her great delight lay in linen thread work.

That night she was absorbed in her task of making beautiful linen table mats. (I still treasure them over seventy years later.) The only light came from a table lamp by her side, but it seemed to me to suffuse her with a magical mist. My bed was in darkness. It was warm: I was on the edge of sleep. Suddenly, I knew I was loved by her in a way I had never been fully conscious of before. It enveloped me with such a feeling of security that I felt that I could face any hardship or suffering that might come to me later in life.

Adult reflections on these ecstatic experiences

Both these moments passed, as all such experiences of ecstasy do, but the memories of them stayed. They have sustained me through the whole of my adult life in all sorts of different and difficult circumstances.

Knowing that one is loved unconditionally is a gift that does not come to all children. It may not come in adult life. We often think we know what it is to love another person or object without reserve, and we may give ourselves without reserve. We adore, sometimes from afar, someone with whom we are intimate. We long to be loved in return; but to know that one is *loveable* is different. It is a gift beyond compare if we learn it from a parent or from an early figure in our childhood. It can, however, come at any time in life and we should never give up hope of receiving it, however low our self-esteem might be. It is not a gift that can be earned: it is a gift that we can, however, refuse to accept.

To know that one is loveable is a human birth right, but many people do not realise that they are loveable at all. They have not experienced that precious gift in a way that they can recognise. They cannot actually remember that they have ever known what it is to be loved. And it is all too easy for adults who have been loved to find such statements incredulous. Some of us are even tempted to respond, "Well, God is the Source of Love: God loves you." But that statement has no meaning unless it is supported by action that convinces a desolate person with low self-esteem that he or she is loveable. And this, as many professional carers will know, is not always easy to accomplish.

Once a person has realised that they are loveable they can then love both themselves and others. In my life experience the discovery of being loveable happened as a child. It also happened when I became an adult. I know that I am fortunate. These experiences changed my character and the way I behaved when I grew to maturity.

I have cited these personal examples that effected radical changes in my attitude to my own life, and enabled me to accept suffering and joy as gateways to new ways of living. These events illustrate the dynamic between despair and hope. They also illustrate events of great joy, akin to ecstasy, that can happen in one person's lifetime. The transformation in that person then affects her future direction. These experiences are akin to 'conversion' experiences, but they are not necessarily confined to religious people or linked to concepts of outside interference from a 'higher being' called God. They are what they are: experiences that are open to different interpretations, only one of which incorporates any notion of deity. Scientists and some people of faith tend to negate these experiences as 'imaginary', but to those of us to whom such events have occurred they are mysterious realities that profoundly affect the direction of our lives.

Teenage years

Life between the ages of nine and fifteen was preoccupied with school work and poverty but, in 1937 or perhaps spring 1938, my mother and I travelled to Latvia for the last time in my childhood. We went via Berlin, where my mother again fell ill. On one of her days of convalescence we went to visit an impoverished artist and his wife. Our friends were extolling the improvements in their lifestyle since Adolph Hitler had come to power. The German nation had suffered from the reprisals inflicted on them by the victorious nations after the First World War had ended in 1918. Hitler's ascent to power in 1934 had given our friends a better life. They were still poor and our staple diet during our visit was cabbage pie with thick and heavy soggy pastry but their morale had improved.

On this particular day Adolph Hitler was giving a speech at a nearby stadium. Through the loud speakers we could hear his high-pitched rapid speech and the cries of adulation as he spoke to a large audience of supporters. I did not understand much German, but the sounds frightened me. During the rest of our visit I can remember my mother speaking approvingly about Hitler's message to 'Aryan Germans' and his denunciation of some 'rich Jewish profiteers'. This did not seem very strange to me for during my pre-teen years I had heard many references to 'filthy Jews' in England where anti-Semitism was common in the environment in which I lived. The same anti-Semitism was also voiced in my Latvian family where my older three cousins, Arthur, Ervin and Harry had joined the Nazi Youth Party. I can also recall during that visit seeing Jews wearing distinctive arm bands in the streets, and being taunted.

When my mother recovered we moved on to the village of Libau close to the Black Sea in Latvia, where we spent August with my elderly English grandmother, her eldest daughter, Mabel, and my three cousins. Arthur and Harry were scarred with duelling scars as signs of their manhood, but Ervin, my favourite cousin was a gentler person altogether and became my friend and hero. I cried when I left Latvia, never to return.

In August 1939, Britain declared war against Germany and our families were split apart. We heard nothing from our Baltic German family until after the war ended in 1945. Arthur and Harry were killed fighting for Germany on the Russian front. Ervin was captured by the Soviet army and imprisoned until after the war. My grandmother died by the roadside as she fled to Germany but my Aunt Mabel and her husband did escape to

Germany where they were welcomed as refugees from Soviet occupation.

My mother and I stayed in London during the first year of the war. We lived in a flat near Hyde Park where the anti-aircraft batteries were stationed and we survived the first bombardments of London, although many of our friends and neighbours were killed. My mother declined to go into nearby underground shelters so we would go downstairs when the air sirens sounded and get ourselves under a table while the house shook and groaned as it was buffeted by falling bombs and cannon fire.

In 1940 we moved to Great Malvern, Worcestershire, to run a guest house for war time workers who were moved to there to live on sites protected from falling bombs by the Malvern range of hills. My mother and I lived in unheated rooms at the top of a large house where we cared for paying guests and billeted workers for the rest of the war.

In Great Malvern I went to a Plymouth Brethren School for a time where I received daily religious teaching of a strict moral kind. Girls wore pigtails and skirts that fell below our knees. We were forbidden to go to the cinema or to engage in other frivolous activities. We were steeped in Bible teaching in the kindest possible way. I loved that school and was very upset when my mother took me away because she did not think I was receiving as good an education as she wanted. I was transferred to Malvern Girls College as a day girl. I was not happy there but I did receive a good education in science.

I grew up into physical maturity in Great Malvern. Bombs fell in Malvern Link, sited in the valley at the bottom end of the town; and from our home we saw the flames during the bombing that destroyed Coventry Cathedral on the night of November 14th-15th 1940. Hardships, rationing, daily news of killing and wounding among our friends accompanied our lives and seemed like pinpricks compared with the sufferings of people in the large towns in the Midlands and southern part of Britain. My mother was also a guardian to two Polish refugee children entrusted to us by their parents who remained in Poland. The children lived with us throughout the war. We dug up the garden, grew food, kept hens, made bread out of war time flour that sometimes tasted of sawdust mixed with wheat, hoarded rations for feasts and did our best to enjoy life while it lasted.

During adolescence I went through the usual turmoil associated with that phase of life. I was exploring who I was, and what I was going to do in my adult life. My mother wanted me to become a medical doctor. It was our way out of our poverty. I fell into line with her plans. At that time our lives were complicated as many of our relatives were living abroad in Latvia, Russia, Germany and Italy. They were enemies of our nation, but they were still beloved in our eyes. In 1944 I was awarded a State Scholarship that enabled me to go to Girton College at Cambridge University to read for a natural science and medical degree.

Falling in love with God

Like most of my generation I had been confirmed into the Church of England at school; on an impulse that went against my mother's dislike of faith institutions. My desire to establish my identity over and against hers, together with peer group conformity, may have contributed to that action: for it was quickly succeeded by a lapse from observance.

In 1945 however, during my initial year at University, I 'fell in love' with God rather than with another human being. This happened soon after I had been overwhelmed by anguish. The agony happened in the middle of a noisy dining room full of undergraduates. I had just been exposed as a liar by a devout Catholic medical student who scoffed at my Church of England membership. She had asserted that non-Catholics did not go to confession. "Yes, they do", I said. "Do you?" "Yes!" I replied. It was a lie. I was ashamed, very ashamed. One of the stern teachings of my mother was that lying was wrong and evil. That lie demanded restitution, so I went to confession as a way of repairing the lie.

I crouched nervously at the back of an Anglo-Catholic church where confessions were being heard. When my turn came I was ignorant of the correct procedure. I cast myself at a startled priest's feet. He gravely pointed to where I should kneel and told me what to do. Once the ordeal was over he asked me to see him outside the confessional so that he could instruct me in the elements of the 'high church' Anglican faith to which he belonged. I agreed and immediately felt a sense of relief which was akin to ecstasy. I had fallen in love with God; or was it the priest? I do not know. The moment passed. In consequence I became an enthusiast and I promptly followed in the way I was taught. 'Falling in love' did not, of course, mean that I was doing anything reasonable, any more than falling in love with one person and not another is reasonable. I was a prisoner of my own humanity and capable of worshipping idols and fantasies at that age, and I did. I have no doubt at all, now that I am old, that my original faith was constructed round an over-zealous compliance to beliefs that contradicted some of the scientific facts and theories that were current among my colleagues and friends in whom I confided. I wanted to believe in God and I was going to do so – whatever anyone said.

I was still at Cambridge University when the first atom bombs fell on Hiroshima on August 6th 1945. We did not understand the horror of that occasion immediately, for we were overtaken with joy at the end of the war. All I can remember about VJ night in Cambridge is the relief we felt as we celebrated the capitulation of the Japanese Emperor. The exposure of the horrors of the Holocaust and the Japanese prisoner camps came later.

Meanwhile for us in England, life did not change all that much. Life continued with many adventures. I gained a half blue for diving from Cambridge University, captained our swimming team the next year, acted as secretary to the Medical Society, watched political debates at the Union and took a full part in the life of my university and church. Medical students were exempt from conscription and crammed their learning into reduced years of study. Rationing continued. I studied, passed my undergraduate exams and received an honorary degree from Cambridge, however; at that time, women were not awarded Cambridge University degrees. Nor, in 1947, could Cambridge medical students be accepted for further training at Addenbrooke's Hospital: so we all had to find further education in different hospitals. I was fortunate enough to be accepted at the London Hospital as one of their first three women students since the end of the 1914-18 war.

Chapter 2

Life after the Second World War

In 1947 I left Cambridge and my tuition as a medical student continued at the London Hospital in the East End of London. Towards the end of the war the government of the day had insisted that all the major London hospitals took 10% of women for their clinical studies so I went there as one of three women, one from Oxford University, one from London University and one from Cambridge University. It was an adventurous ride for us because the innovative change was not welcomed by all the male students or by some of their teachers. We three women survived the teasing and discriminations that went on at that time and we all managed to qualify in January 1951.

It was at the London Hospital that I first encountered the incredible kindness and generosity of heart of the consultants towards some of their impoverished patients. Their example touched me deeply. Their representative in this personal memoir is Dr A E Clark-Kennedy, one of the eminent physicians of the time. He used to bring some of his patients into his hospital wards at Christmas time for some special treatment. During the five years that I was a medical student and junior doctor he would dispense their treatment regimes, but he would also write them up for sherry (as a medicine) and give them a wonderful time at Christmas in a warm ward, heated by an open fire. I have often wondered since then whether that was a feature of 'benign charity' before the advent of the National Health Service (4) or a universal provision of humane and holistic medical treatment. But these humane attitudes have prevailed among many of the caring professionals I have met since I qualified, although in recent times they sometimes seem to have become overlaid by a desire for financial efficiency that takes precedence over human care and sometimes causes undue delays in treatment, rapid discharges from hospital and poorly coordinated treatments in post-hospital community care. The training at the London Hospital, however, has stayed with me throughout my own professional life.

Life as a medical student was a combination of excitement, nervousness at learning new skills and a good deal of teasing from medical students and teachers alike. At first we three women were excluded from the undergraduate male common room and from 'Mess nights' where the men indulged in what they called 'dirty stories not fit for women's ears'. But we had our own way of telling similar 'girlie' stories in our own enclave where we laughed at our male colleagues and caricatured some of our teachers in cruel ways. When the next year's input of women students arrived we gradually integrated into the communal life typical of students the world over even though some discriminatory practices were still carried out against women students. The 'first three' women graduated successfully and I qualified in January 1951 and joined the new team of junior house officers.

It was during my time as a house officer that I fell in love with an overseas fellow doctor and committed adultery. Our love affair was brief, as we knew it would be: for six months later he returned to his home country and his wife. I was left with my conscience. I withdrew from social activities and focused on work. I was clever, too clever, maybe, but at that time all women had to be unusual to gain admission to medical school and I was ambitious. I remained a house officer for nearly two years and set my mind to becoming a neurosurgeon, despite being warned by my training neurosurgical consultant, Mr D W C Northfield (5), that I would have to remain single if I wanted to undertake such a difficult 'course to the top'. That did not surprise me. By that time I had returned to the practice of my faith and was under the guidance of my Franciscan friar; so celibacy did not seem at all strange to me. I simply decided that men were out of bounds.

I was enjoying my life as a house officer when an unusual event occurred towards the end of my post-graduate training at the London Hospital when I was appointed to a urological team whose consultant was on the point of retirement. The retiring surgeon refused to have me on his team because he thought I would 'upset' his male patients. So I was sent on 'gardening leave' for three weeks until his retirement. I joined a two-week long Franciscan Mission in the town of Chippenham, near Bristol with a team of Anglican friars and young lay people, led by my priest Br Denis Marsh SSF(6). I do not know how the Mission affected the people of Chippenham, but I do know that during the two weeks I met my 'mysterious force' again and was turned upside down by the event. I came to the conclusion that, if I had to remain single, as many women doctors before me had done, I might as well abandon my ambitions and become a nun who was also a doctor, available to serve as a missionary.

This decision was headstrong. It was opposed by my mother who was then living in Paris, by my father then living in Germany, by professors and teachers at the hospital, by many of my friends and some of the priest advisors I turned to for advice. In the end there was no stopping me. I got on a train by myself and went off. It might have seemed ridiculous but I was persuasive at all the interviews I attended at two different convents and in the end I was accepted as a postulant at a large Anglican Missionary Order where my advisors thought that I might still have had a reasonable chance of practising medicine later on. That was not in my plans for I had wanted to join a strictly enclosed, reputably austere, Order dedicated to prayer and hard work. In the end, however, I accepted the compromise obediently.

To Africa

I joined the Anglican Community of the Holy Name (7) that was located in my home town of Malvern just before Christmas in 1953. I spent two years in the novitiate and was professed in simple vows in 1955. I did not have an easy novitiate because I had missed medical practice so I went to Liberia with a strong conviction that I had a double vocation to the religious life and to medicine. Then our Mother Superior sent me back to the London Hospital for a refresher course and transferred me to their African out-station in Liberia where the resident male doctor had been recalled to America. He belonged to the American Anglican Order of the Holy Cross (8): the Order had founded the Mission village where our Community served.

In Africa all went well for a time, although there were tensions from the beginning as I had to be dispensed from some Eucharistic services and other convent duties in order to be able to operate early in the mornings before the heat of the day made such work too exhausting to continue. Being a woman doctor was an advantage: in the village of Bolahun where we worked, men were not allowed to attend women during childbirth. In that region certain endemic illnesses affected the cervixes of women, making them so inelastic that the cervixes would not open to allow a baby to be born. Formerly these women died. Being a woman, I was allowed into the birthing hut. I was also able to operate under spinal anaesthesia, and so I delivered twelve women by Caesarean section. I had asked my Community to let me know in good time if they wanted to recall me to England because I was concerned for these twelve women. I hoped to offer to sterilise these mothers if my replacement was a man. As an Anglican I would have had no difficulty with that decision.

Unfortunately I became involved in another crisis, probably because I was too imbued with Christian ideals. In our area there was considerable competition between the local Liberian 'medicine men' and our kind of Western medicine. I was called out to see a powerful local chief who was also a 'medicine man'. He was so ill that I brought him into our hospital for treatment.

He died. I was blamed for his death. Had I been more experienced I might have realised what might happen in consequence. Subsequently, there was considerable trouble in our neighbourhood. Hostility towards the Christian missionaries continued. The resident Christian staff had more experience than I. They were worried: so were the Superiors of two religious communities, one in America, one in England. The result was that the Superior of the American Order of the Holy Cross, Fr Leopold Kroll OHC, came to resolve the disputes. At the end of a two-month investigation he decided that I should return to our Mother House in England.

The news was most unwelcome to me, but there was nothing I could do about it. But I had to wait for several weeks before my return home could be arranged. During this time my twelve Caesarean mothers began to haunt my mind and I became unable to work. I became unbalanced in my thinking. I was cared for by staff, and significantly by, Jembe, a 'white witch' with whom I had become friends. Jembe ran the girls' bush school during which she circumcised girls at puberty. Although this practice was horrific to my way of thinking, I could do nothing to stop it, so I gave Jembe acriflavine for their wounds and we exchanged our medical knowledge. Our friendship helped her to stop babies from dying from the tetanus caused by bacteria carried in the mud that was plastered on the babies' umbilical cord stumps and so was able to help Jembe to understand there was a safer way.

Jembe was a wise woman. She came and sat with me when I was ill: she foresaw that the conflict in me between my Christian religious vows and my medical vocation would lead me to another crisis of conscience. It did. Medicine won; and from that point onwards I knew that I would leave the Order when I got back to England. The monk who had come out to sort out the political mess I had unwittingly caused, Leopold Kroll, decided that I was still too ill to travel alone and so he escorted me to

Paris where my mother and his brother lived. He had cared for me spiritually during my nervous breakdown.

In Paris both of us discovered that we were not suited to continue in the religious life. We wrote to our respective Orders to tell them of our intention to marry. It caused ructions in both our Orders and the Anglican Church. I was still ill and fragile. The monk, Leo, would not leave me, despite desperate attempts to save his vocation: for he was in life vows. My vows were only temporary; so no one tried to rescue me.

Marriage

On June 1st, 1957 we married in a registry office in Birmingham, England. Leo was twenty-five years older than I. He was dismissed from his Order and was blacklisted by the then Archbishop of Canterbury: meaning that he could not take any paid employment as a priest. I had to become the main wage earner, while he took a low paid lay job to help us to survive. We accepted our punishment. I found a job as a junior doctor in an urban medical practice in Tooting, South West London. We stayed there until our eldest child was eight months old.

It was in south London that I first met a fairly large number of immigrants from British colonies, and learnt about the problems they were encountering during their attempts to integrate into a very different way of life in the 'mother country'. At that time many of my women patients were Hindus and some were Muslims. Many brought their husbands or children with them because they generally could not speak English. Somehow, without my telling them, they knew that I was a person of religious faith, like them, but different. That knowledge made a strong bond between us as we exchanged greetings and communicated by gesture more than speech. I was happy in that work. However, Leo was a dedicated African missionary. He wanted to return to that continent, but to a different country. So, after the birth of our eldest daughter Florence in 1958, we went to Namibia with the help of the United Society for the Propagation of the Gospel. We were overjoyed to be working in Namibia, but this time I was a different person.

In Liberia I had been a nun, a single woman. While I was there I did not worry about my own life and safety. I tackled and killed snakes and scorpions. I went on periodic long treks to visit leper colonies and coped with all kinds of tropical dangers, including a local smallpox epidemic. In Namibia I was the mother of an infant daughter, and I was also pregnant with my second child, our son, Leopold. We lived in an area that suffered from periodic drought and crop failures. It was also a village where rabid dogs ran freely about our compound and where diseases like tuberculosis were rife. Namibia was a South African protectorate and the apartheid laws were strictly observed, though there was an active liberation movement against them. We also lived close to a war area on the border of Angola.

This time I could not cope with the fears that came with motherhood. When, in 1961, we were eventually expelled from the Mission station because we had unwittingly broken some of the apartheid laws. I was secretly glad to be going home to England. On the way home I fell ill again, this time with the ill effects of the drugs I was taking to prevent malaria. I had to be hospitalised. When we arrived in England we had nothing. All our possessions had been left behind. My mother was still living in France. My father, then living in Germany, lent us a hut in the Ashdown forest until I fully recovered and was able to take up work in General Practice. I settled into this work. My husband found work in a lay capacity: it was not well paid. My work involved several moves for our family between 1961 and 1987 when my husband died.

We worked on several housing estates in Outer London and Surrey where there was considerable social deprivation brought about by moving whole communities from the slum areas of South London into newly built housing estates in the suburbs. In

the slum areas there had been close links with family and neighbours, but in these new estates these links were broken.
Moreover, many women who lived in high-rise flats were
mistreated by their husbands and partners, mainly through
domestic violence as the result of alcohol and drugs. Illegal
abortions were common. Women sometimes died or were
mutilated. Their plight and illnesses were treated with disdain. It
was during my early life as a general medical practitioner in
England that the plight of women who had died in Liberia, for
whom I had been able to do virtually nothing, returned to my
memory. The memories alerted me to the plight of some of my
British women patients. This time I was able to act more
positively.

One of my young mothers, aged twenty-nine with three
young children, came to me with persistent vaginal bleeding and
other suspicious symptoms and signs. I sent her to our local
hospital. She and I were told that there "was nothing wrong with
her. She is an overanxious fussy woman." Nine months later she
died from rampant cervical cancer. I was devastated because at
that time cervical cytology was available as a diagnostic tool in
some areas, and it was also available to private patients in our
area, but not to patients who could not afford to pay. My anger
led to action. I went to King's College hospital to be trained as a
cytologist, obtained a medical research grant to buy the necessary
equipment and set up a cytology service in my practice. I
continued this work until our local hospital set up its own service
and then turned my attention to other issues that caused me and
other professional women working in our area to feel that we
needed to try and change the laws that discriminated unjustly
against women and others.

From early on in my medical work here I noticed that
homosexual men were coming to see me because of their fears of
being blackmailed, exposed and prosecuted for their behaviour.
Before the Law was changed in 1967 homosexual acts between

consenting adults were deemed to be criminal. But I began to study psychiatry and so moved from condemnation into thinking of homosexuality as an illness. This further research altered my opinion, convinced me that homosexuality was a normal variant in gender identity and helped me to understand the nature of the fears and depressive illnesses that some of my homosexual patients were suffering from through persecution on account of their condition.

At the same time, spurred on by the decision of the Lambeth Conference of 1968 that there were no theological objections to the ordination of women to the threefold ministries of the Anglican Church, I began my training to be a deaconess. I felt that some women who had been deeply hurt by men needed women pastors who could understand their emotional and spiritual difficulties more empathically than a male priest. I thought that the Church of England would respond to this need with generosity. Maybe I should have known better, but I did not. I also realised that some homosexual men and women might need more spiritual and pastoral care than I was qualified to give.

At this stage of my life I had no idea of the consequence of this desire to train as a non-stipendiary deaconess, nor of the resulting radicalisation that took me from a happy and relatively quiet life as a wife, mother and local medical practitioner into a wider and more challenging role as a Christian socio-political activist.

Chapter 3

Learning Skills for New Challenges

In 1970, after three years of training on the Southwark Ordination Course as the only woman among twenty men, all of whom were training for priesthood, I was made a non-stipendiary deaconess. During these training years I was fully supported by my husband who had originally laughed at me when I first suggested that my and other women's sense of vocation to the priesthood should be tested by the Anglican Church. He changed his mind when he saw how differently I was treated from my male fellow students. During my training I was ineligible for book grants because I was not going to be ordained: so the other students clubbed together and gave me a grant. For the whole of the first year I was not allowed to sleep in the same building as the men at residential weekends and so had to commute some fifty miles back and forth from home each Friday after I finished my evening surgery, during the early morning and late evening on Saturday and then again early on Sunday morning so as to arrive in time for the morning Eucharist by 7.00am. Consciously or unconsciously the training Course had made it hard for me to continue to study, but the obstacles made Leo and I more determined to persevere, and with his help I did. After the first year things got a little easier for I was boarded out near the Course residence during our two-week Summer School, while my husband looked after our four children. Then, in our second year the restrictions were removed. Thankfully, today's ordinands do not have to go through such difficulties.

In 1970 I was made a deaconess in Southwark Cathedral at the same service as my fellow students who were ordained to the diaconate and would go on to the priesthood a year later. The service was solemn. There were three ordaining bishops present to lay hands on the male candidates' heads and to intone the ritual words of ordination, imploring the Holy Spirit to 'send grace' to the new deacons. I was at the end of a long line of kneeling men and when the bishops came to lay hands on me, they prayed; but somehow the Holy Spirit knew He was not to descend on me because I was a woman. I remained a lay person authorised by the Church of England to exercise the ministry of a lay deaconess.

Little did I know what would be the outcome of that ministry. I simply imagined I could do youth work and help our vicar in some of his pastoral work. I also hoped I could become a pastor to women with family problems. But my vicar in Chislehurst, who had initially supported my desire to train for ministry, declined my offer of help at the end of my studies. I had to move to another diocese to find a priest who would accept me as a deaconess and we had to move house and work. The Revd Donald Reeves accepted us into his parish. I worked with him for ten years and we have remained long-time friends (9).

Activist

In 1972 the government of the day published a white paper suggesting that they would remove family allowances that were paid to mothers and transfer them into fathers' pay packets. My health visitor and I knew that most of that transferred money would never reach the women and children. So we decided to join a protest rally in Hyde Park. I thought that other Christians would be going and rang twenty charities who were concerned with women and children. I was told that the charities did not join in 'women's lib' demonstrations. I had never before heard of 'women's lib' or 'bra-burning'. But I put on my deaconess uniform and sallied forth to the rally. There I found other ordinary housewives and working women; and I found other Christian women concerned about disadvantaged people in society. We marched peacefully, sang songs, and found one another. That was when I became a Christian activist. After that rally, I and others founded the Christian Parity Group to promote the partnership of women and men rather than dominion by one sex over the other. The Group included men and women and worked alongside secular feminist organisations to change discriminatory practices against women in society. It was not a charity so we could engage in socio-political work.

In 1974, at the request of Women in Media and the journalist, Mary Stott (10), I stood for election to a parliamentary seat in a marginal constituency in Sutton, Surrey. My agent was Jewish. One of my chief helpers in this venture was Donald Reeves, the vicar of the Church to which I was attached. Other supporters included a well-known actress, who later became a Labour MP, a woman feminist who later became a Conservative MP, and a woman journalist who worked on a Communist newspaper. We had a remarkable campaign in Sutton, attracted the headlines because we were in a marginal seat, and ended up with three hundred votes. It was a magnificent failure that had captured media attention. We had helped to persuade all the major parties to say they would support the Sex Discrimination Bill then going through its British parliamentary procedures to become law in 1975.

The plight of my African mothers, of my patients in England, and of my own difficulties during my training to become a deaconess, had all contributed to my radicalisation, but had also given me my vocation as a minister of the Church of England. My public life had begun, but without my realising its full implications to our personal lives. I continued my socio-political work for disadvantaged women, both in my own country and in the World Council of Churches and the Christian Medical Commission for a number of years.

As a medical doctor in general medical practice I was treated by patients and colleagues alike as a well-informed and responsible adult. I was qualified to give advice, offer prescriptions to assist healing, refer patients to consultant specialists in hospital and care for those who were ill and dying. In these respects I was the equal of male doctors. Being a woman was a disadvantage in regard to income and opportunities for advancement, but I was not excluded from any part of my professional work. I was well aware that I was spared from most of the greater disadvantages suffered by many women in the sexist British society of that time, except that, like every other woman of my generation, I was not allowed to incur debt. My unemployed husband had to sign my hire purchase debt documents. He was humiliated and felt himself to be an inadequate person. I raged, but complied with the law because we needed a new gas cooker.

As a deaconess, I was *not* treated as an equal but different colleague. Being a woman in the Church of England's ministry at that time meant being excluded from much of the work of the ordained male clergy. My ministry was restricted to helping my male parish priest in whatever he gave me to do. I could not preside or preach at Holy Communion (11). I could not take a funeral without the express permission of the vicar and the mourners and few gave that permission. Relatively few women were prominent in the decision-making processes of the Church of England, certainly not a newly made deaconess who volunteered her services in a local parish. Like most women of my age group, I was used to this attitude of the Church. I did not, however, agree with it.

Becoming a deaconess in 1970 had other consequences for I began to meet theological and moral challenges in my medical practice. There was a difference between the traditional Christian teaching of the Anglican Church to which I converted and the relational and moral difficulties of some of my patients who sought my advice. One of our neighbouring practices was staffed by Catholic doctors and, around this time, some of their patients, also Catholics, began to come to me for discussions about their moral attitudes towards contraception. Some also came seeking abortion. I had no difficulty with contraceptive advice since my Anglican Church was not opposed to it. I had more trouble with some requests for abortion since I was not in favour of abortion on demand and yet my experiences with women who had formerly had 'back street abortions' prompted me not to opt out of supporting David Steel's 1967 Abortion Act; though that was contentious in principle for many.

At that time I had virtually no other Christian women ministers with whom to discuss these issues. Most of the male priests I knew at the time had 'black and white' attitudes that emphasised principles rather than practical issues to do with real life compassion. I had to make decisions alone and I often got them wrong. An episode from my medical experiences at this time illustrates this tension between my Christian views and morality and the practical difficulties that were afflicting marriage in my encounters with real live people.

At odds with the Church

From before the decriminalisation of homosexuality in 1967 onwards my patients also included many homosexuals who were in trouble. Originally I, like many other doctors of my time thought of homosexuality as an illness rather than a crime. Active homosexual behaviour between adults was still listed as such in the directory of psychiatric illnesses. I, however, was now meeting some active homosexuals who had lived as loving and faithful partners for over thirty years, one of whom was himself a consultant child psychiatrist. I could not see any signs of illness in this couple, nor could I detect it in many other women and men who were living in irregular relationships. Any illness in many of these people seemed to be due to depression arising from their fears of exposure, blackmail, prosecution, and imprisonment. So I began to read about the subject both from a theological a psychological point of view.

After considerable research I stopped recommending psychological 'reversion therapies'. I began to read literature by
homosexual people and to listen to them in a different way. I
concluded that they were right to regard themselves as a normal
significant minority of the human population with genetic
predispositions to same-sex sex attraction. From that point on I
supported all efforts to change the Law and to decriminalise
private adult homosexual behaviour.

My support was contrary to the official teaching of the Church
of England and to that of the Catholic Church. This was the first
time that I made a conscientious decision to dissent from the
Christian teaching I had received before I was made a deaconess.
As a result some old and new friends became active members of
the Christian Parity Group, and we refused to deal with women-
only issues, but contested discriminatory practices against
homosexuals as well. The Group was not popular with those who
wanted us to concentrate only on discrimination against women
and our prime focus remained the equal partnership of women
and men. But together with other people and organisations, we
began to try to change the laws of the Church and State that
discriminated against women, purely on account of their gender.
At that time our impatient logic suggested that such changes
could be made quite quickly. However, our supporters warned us
that it was going to be a long haul. It was protracted in both the
Church and society and, indeed, in Britain institutional sexism is
still present.

In all this work I was fully supported by my husband. During
my early years as a deaconess I, and another much younger
Welsh deaconess, Linda Mary Evans, were the only people who
confessed to our sense of being called to ministerial priesthood.
Many others came forward later, but in those first few years we
were alone and, consequently, of interest to the media. It was not
an easy time for our family of growing children and we all
suffered from the notoriety. Leo and I used to pray together on

many occasions to see if we ought to stop our activism; on each occasion we felt that God wanted us to continue. ·

The call to priesthood

Some other women felt the call to priesthood, but kept quiet lest they be labelled as arrogant to consider such a dreadful thing. They could and did campaign for other women to become priests, but not themselves. Some of these women were remarkable people who were campaigning long before my time in quiet ways and producing good intellectual arguments in support of the ordination of women. Along with all present-day women priests, I owe a great debt of gratitude to people like my great friend, Deaconess Elsie Baker. She worked tirelessly as a deaconess long before I came on the scene, suffered the discrimination, brought up an adopted daughter by herself in the days when that was very difficult to do. She was a patient woman who put up with my own impatience and later joined me and others in keeping prayer vigils outside Church House on occasions when the General Synod of the Church of England were debating issues to do with the ordination of women to the diaconate and priesthood.

The Christian Parity Group proactively courted media publicity and gave financial support to two women ordinands, Kath Burn and Elisabeth Canham, who went to America for their studies and were ordained over there. It welcomed women priests from overseas, like the Revds Susan Cole-King, and Sister Mary Michael Simpson, OSH, an American nun, when they visited us in England and submitted to our ecclesiastical laws but witnessed to their priesthood in public.

I travelled abroad to America on several occasions to New York, Louisiana, Minneapolis and Minnesota to promote our ideas among deaconesses and at Nonconformist conferences. During those times I met some of the women in the American Episcopal Church, and the Anglican Church in Canada, New

Zealand and Australia who were working towards ordination. Although in some ways the Christian Parity Group was more concerned with the plight of women in society, all our members realised that women were baptised members of the established Church of our country and believed they could represent God in ordained ministries as well as their male counterparts. That is why we participated in Church activism, just as we were doing with regard to equal pay and equal opportunities for women and men. The two areas of work were seen to be equally important symbolically, though different because of the theological arguments about the nature of the Church.

It was during one of my travels to New York that I was challenged by an encounter with an American Roman Catholic nun who was attending the same Deaconess Conference in 1972 as I was, though I was not there as a representative Anglican deaconess. While I was there I attended a Methodist Service of Holy Communion, presided over by a woman minister. I remember being troubled as to whether or not I should take Holy Communion from her hands since she had not been ordained by an Anglican bishop. To my amazement my nun friend got up and moved towards the altar. I followed her, received the Sacrament, and returned to my seat. My bonds with traditional ideas about continuity of the validity of Holy Orders through historic succession in the episcopacy were weakening, just as my own inherited prejudice against women priests that lay deep under my outward support for the principle of women's ordination was also being challenged by overseas Anglican women priests, including Li Tim Oi (12), and Joyce Bennett (13), ordained in Hong Kong in 1944 and 1971, and by the first Canadian and American women priests ordained in their own Anglican Churches in 1972.

By the time that I left the Deaconess Conference in America I had received the sacraments of Reconciliation and Holy Communion from the hands of overseas Anglican women priests.

When I returned to England I continued to break the rules and learnt to feel confident about participating in Nonconformist services, and was even more convinced that we needed women priests in the Church of England. I was also more committed to the 'ginger group' nature of the Christian Parity Group that was more active than other organisations. We were beginning to demonstrate more openly in England whenever we could, knowing that we would cause irritation, opposition and condemnation. We set out to capture the headlines and we succeeded.

Leading a double life

The years between 1972 and 1978 were full of engagements outside my medical practice. I belonged to good medical partnerships and was supported by my colleagues provided I fulfilled my duties effectively. Leo and I managed, but at a considerable cost to our family. We depended on my income from medical work and it was during those years that I learnt to combine the theological and psychological skills gained through further study.

It was also then that I changed the way I worked as a doctor since I had a radical Christian socialist vicar in the Revd Donald Reeves who worked in a different way from most Anglican vicars of his time. Donald's influence was formative in the development of my lay ministry. At the time both of us were also influenced by the theologians who initiated 'liberation theologies' in South America such as the Peruvian Gustavo Gutierrez (14). Donald was one of the priests in the Southwark Diocese who were developing what was then called South Bank Theology: in practice, a way of sharing authority with lay people in impoverished areas of London (15). He challenged me over the way I used my medical authority in an 'I know best' sort of a way in my interactions with the impoverished and socially deprived people in the areas where I worked.

I can best illustrate this tussle between the South Bank radical theology represented by my vicar, and the traditional training I had received as a middle class doctor of medicine by describing what happened in my locality as a result of trying to reconcile both disciplines. At the time I was serving a large area of South Wimbledon that overlapped with our parish church boundaries.

My 'double role' as medical doctor and deaconess meant that I might sign the death certificate of a patient on one day, and reappear in the same household a few days later as a deaconess prepared to take the funeral of the deceased. The family and I had known each other and lived with the dying person's suffering for weeks, months, or even years. I had witnessed all that they had witnessed. But when I appeared as a deaconess, it was as if they thought of me as a completely different person. To them, the medical doctor's work was finished, so they simply ignored my previous role. They needed to tell the story to a new person, one who had seemingly not been there during the dying process. So I would hear it all over again, but from a different perspective. I would hear what the doctor had done and said as if they did not know that it was I whom they were speaking about. This had its challenging side sometimes for, in listening to their accounts, I realised that I had plainly not communicated properly with them at the time of their need despite thinking I had done so. And often the 'district' and Macmillan nurses came in for a great deal more praise than I did. And that was a salutary lesson for me!

The service that I did provide as a deaconess to some of my patients during those ten years taught me a great deal about death and grief. It taught me to listen, and listen, and listen again without comment, but with sympathy and even sometimes with empathy. The families needed compassion and space to vent their own feelings of anger, resentment and abandonment without being judged. They generally needed a dispassionate and patient listener: not one who would empathise to the extent of being so involved in the grief that they sought to end it by comforting words of their own. They needed someone with time to spare and, all too often, those in authority were perceived to be just too busy to spare the time. Astonishingly, it was as a deaconess that I had time to spare simply because, as a lay person, I was understood to have virtually no authority.

My experience of being a deaconess together with my theological conversations helped me to understand the importance of my 'double role' – where neither role was suppressed as it had been when I was a nun in Africa. The powerlessness of the deaconess role was an important lesson to the doctor in me. I began to exercise a more collaborative way of working with patients, asking them for their input into our work together, allowing them to disagree with me, even when I disagreed with their decisions. Open communication about treatments became more important than a previously mysterious aura of authority gained through superior professional knowledge. We learnt to become partners in the search for health. Moreover, I became less intolerant when they dissented from my kind of allopathic medicine and consulted alternative practitioners such as osteopaths, acupuncturists, hypnotherapists, teachers of transcendental meditation, yoga teachers and faith healers. I wrote an article in the Times about Transcendental Meditation and in 1974 I published my first book TM – *A Signpost for the World'*(16).

My venture into writing as a medical doctor and as a Christian minister initiated me into a new career as a Christian medical author which has continued for the rest of my life. My passion to combine modern scientific knowledge with what I consider to be core truths about Christianity has led to attempts to communicate with others who do not see science and Christian theology to be incompatible. Since 1974 I have published thirteen books on various medical and social features of human living. (See Appendix.)

The lifestyle that Leo and I adopted could not have been

possible had both of us been working full time. During these years Leo became more of a house partner than a working father. I had been gifted by birth with an astonishing energy and a relatively small need for sleep, something that many of my friends and colleagues found difficult to deal with. That energy, I think, came from the Temple family genes, from my grand-mother's forebears. So I worked long hours, wrote at night, slept for three or four hours, woke with renewed energy and managed to use short spells of time during each day with unusual focus of attention to the present moment. I could be described as a 'jack of all trades, but master of none' or as a polymath who tended to wear other colleagues out. But this lifestyle was costly to our family. My growing children found it difficult to have a broad-casting, campaigning mother. I found it difficult to continue, but whenever we discussed 'pulling out' we found ourselves unable to do so; not least because we depended on my income from medical practice.

At this period I was becoming a thorn in the flesh of many members of the Church of England who considered my behaviour to be aggressively unladylike. Little did they know of my fears about the cost of our work to everyone who was willing 'to stand up and be counted'. Many of the women who were brave enough to belong to the Christian Parity Group suffered from the criticisms we attracted. Some became ill with depression that followed massive rejection and ridicule. Some lost their faith and left the Anglican Communion. Some had to withdraw from any campaign activities. Kath Burn and Elisabeth Canham had a hard time in exile from their families during their training for the priesthood in America. They and the Revd Susan Cole King and Sr Mary Michael who came to give preaching and speaking tours in England were positively influential although they were unable to exercise their priesthood in England. We in the British Christian Parity Group and our secular feminist colleagues were thankful to these intrepid supporters for their willingness to suffer what they did at the hands of some detractors. We knew the consequences. We also knew that the quieter campaigning organisations would have to keep their distance from us and get on with their good work. Yet a considerable number of us were able to remain friends despite the differences in our methods.

This educational campaigning work towards the ordination of women was done by the quieter work of organisations like The Anglican Group for the Ordination of Women (AGOW) and its successor, the Movement for the Ordination of Women, (MOW), now renamed WATCH (Women and the Church). I and others also felt supported by The Society for the Ministry of Women (SMWC) which included Methodist and Nonconformist ordained ministers.

Christian Howard, Betty Ridley, Deaconess Diana McClatchley, Ruth and Mollie Batten, Margaret Roxborough, Diana Collins, Margaret Webster, Margaret Davies and a host of other men and women, clergy and lay people, all worked from within the heart of the Church of England to promote women's ordination. Their story, and its successful outcome has been well told by Margaret Webster (17). Twenty-first-century women priests all over the world owe a great debt of gratitude to these quiet pioneers.

Broadening horizons

Meantime the years between 1972 and 1978 were fruitful ones that saw me travelling to conferences in different European countries, Sri Lanka and several parts of the United States of America for speaking engagements. I learnt a great deal from people of different nationalities, cultures and religions. They taught me to be respectful of different ways of thinking from my own. The people I met were closely connected with peace and justice movements in their own countries and they were forward-looking in regard to the environment and population growth. Many of the women I met were only just beginning to be active in public life and we had much to learn from one another.

In 1974 I attended a special meeting in Berlin organised by the World Council of Churches to help women leaders from all over the world to gain confidence and skills in speaking publically. The following year I went as a special advisor, not as a delegate, to the World Council of Churches Assembly in Nairobi and learned how to participate in complex gatherings of Church leaders. I also became a member of the Christian Medical Commission, an international sub-division of the World Council of Churches (18). It was my work with these organisations in the 1970s and 1980s that had the most influence on me. As a member of the Commission I became aware of how people from developing parts of the world were handicapped through their dependence on Western nations for healthcare, particularly in regard to the purchase of drugs.

My work on the Medical Commission took me back to an earlier time in my life. When I was a very young house doctor in one of my first jobs in London, we used a new drug called Chloromycetin for obstinate infections that did not yield to drugs like penicillin and its variants. One of my patients, a young girl of twelve years of age, was given Chloromycetin for a kidney infection. She was our first patient to develop aplastic anaemia after taking this drug. She died. The drug, useful as it was in skin infections and eye infections, was taken off the list of approved drugs for oral use in Britain. But some thirty years later the Commission found that the Western-based drug companies were still selling it to less well-developed countries for oral use. This happened before the developing countries of the world won the right to manufacture their own drugs more cheaply than they could be bought from international drug cartels. Through this Commission I became aware of the educational work undertaken by the World Health Organisation towards the eradication of diseases that were due to malnutrition, inadequate and contaminated water supplies, malaria and other diseases. Having worked in a highly privileged country I became better informed about the effects of poverty, land and water deprivation on the health of indigenous people in other less advantaged parts of our world. In a sense I knew too much: for I was too far down the scale of the world scene to have much influence, but those years taught me the value of prayerful engagement in socio-political affairs.

A price to pay

By 1978 I was a fairly well-known Christian feminist, an advocate for women priests in the Church of England, and an ecumenically-minded activist in inter-denominational and inter-national circles. But the years of struggle with opponents to our collective ideas about the place of women in society and in the Church had taken their toll. People on both sides of the argument, whom I respected, admired and loved, had been wounded by my convictions and actions. My personal involvement in the struggle for partnership with men in social and religious institutions had brought out weaknesses in my own character. The struggles had exposed many of my own prejudices and my aggressive potential. In 1978, when General Synod rejected a motion urging the Church of England to begin the legal process towards accepting women priests I shouted from the gallery: "We asked you for bread and you gave us a stone." I was angry, very angry and I knew it. Sue Dowell, a member of the Christian Parity Group, bravely stood with me to give me support.

My remarks made the headlines. Such behaviour was 'unseemly and unladylike'. It earned me some ostracism among my opponents, and even from many of my supporters. I did not like their condemnation; but I did realise that if I continued to be a prominent advocate I would harm the cause I was espousing, so I began to withdraw from leadership in several spheres of activity. I felt it was time to retire from publicity and let other younger, less tarnished women continue.

A year later my husband became very ill after a stroke. He had been a great supporter of my work in both the Church and society. His illness was life-changing for both of us. We decided to leave our London home and moved to the village of Fairlight Cove in East Sussex where I had spent part of my childhood. I took a lower paid job as a community doctor so that I could give more time to the care of my husband. Our four children were adults by this time and they stayed in London, but we remained in touch through weekend and holiday visits to us in our country home.

I remained an active non-stipendiary worker deaconess, but I was aware that I could no longer go on being upfront in any kind of campaign: besides, I needed to come to terms with my own misandry, aggressive attitudes and behaviour: a task that took nearly seven years to accomplish. During this time I worked as a school doctor monitoring the health of children and supporting families with disabled or disadvantaged children. I served on a multidisciplinary team to counter child abuse through cruelty, violence and sexual assault. There were some wonderful community doctors, school nurses, social workers, policemen and police women in that team and I loved the work. When I left my active work as a campaigner, and simultaneously lost my ability to prescribe as a medical doctor, my emotional strength declined. I was about to pay a price for my years of public exposure and disappointment.

Chapter 4

Crashing into Disbelief and Bereavement

In 1980, aged 54, I came to an unpleasant 'full stop'; a kind of spiritual breakdown. Yes, I had struggled with doubt during my life of faith, but I had ignored those doubts. It is possible that the behaviour of Church officials towards women who, like me, felt called to priestly ordination had gradually weakened my trust in corporate hierarchical authority. It is possible that this gradual distrust in the teaching authority of the Church had gone on for a number of years and had weakened my faith in God, but I had taken no notice. The event, when it happened, came as a complete surprise to me.

I awoke one morning in 1980 to discover that all belief in a loving God, a creator God, a redeemer God, a living Holy Trinity, had vanished almost as suddenly as it had appeared when I was nineteen years old. I thought this feeling of emptiness, or 'non-relationship', would pass. I had read about other people to whom this sort of thing had happened, but who had subsequently recovered, leaving them more faithful than ever. But the darkness did not go away. Week after week, month after month, year after year, I could not locate God in any way that I could recognise as valid. Christian friends, older and more experienced than I, urged me to 'remain faithful'. Bewildered, but still compliant with their advice, I continued to function as a medical doctor and remained an advocate for disadvantaged people. Leo's health was gradually declining, but he remained a firm supporter of all my work and was a 'tower of strength' to me. He, too, urged me to ignore my feelings and to act trustingly in God's existence. I made a deliberate decision to do so and the darkness became for me my way of pilgrimage.

For the next seven years, I felt like an 'empty shell', but I continued to go to church and do all the usual things that Christians do. My reason for doing this was my desire to go on believing in the face of unbelief, and to trust my spiritual advisors. I also wanted to support my Christian women friends who still believed in their vocations to the Anglican priesthood, as indeed I did during small moments of renewed faith. The only way I felt able to do this was to undertake to 'live *as if* there was God'. After all, I did not know there was no God. I only *felt* like an atheist. During those long years very few people knew of my struggle with doubt, aridity and emptiness.

Life after 1979 when we moved to Fairlight in East Sussex was quite different from life in London before my husband's stroke earlier that year. I was no longer a prescribing medical doctor. I had become a community doctor in Hastings. I was living in Chichester diocese in the Church of England where, at that time, women deacons and deaconesses were decidedly unwelcome, although tolerated to some extent for the limited amount of work they were permitted to do. Consequently I was no longer as busy as I had been.

At this time the people who began to come and see me personally for counsel were no longer patients of mine. They were more often marginalised people, non-observant or lapsed Christians, or morally compromised people who were in some sort of difficult conflict situation. I did not choose these people. They just began to appear on my doorstep. Leo and I offered hospitality, a quiet place where people could talk and a non-judgemental approach to their troubles; he through friendship and prayer, I through counsel and prayer.

We had more time to spare in Fairlight Cove than in London. Moreover, I made friends with some wonderful community nurses, especially Janet Davies: together we created a Listening Post for young adolescents, where they could freely discuss their sexual lives, and where they could be referred, if necessary, to one of my medical friends, Dr Mary Rees, who worked in our local Community Health Centre. As a community school doctor my eyes were being opened to a multitude of consequences of poverty and social deprivation, including cruelty and sexual abuse of children, alcoholism and addictions of various kinds, as well as relationship and identity problems. This work began in Fairlight and continued after Leo died in 1987.

I remained an active deaconess in Chichester Diocese and was subsequently elected to be a diocesan representative in General Synod. For by that time I had overcome my misandry and felt safe to give witness and to speak without malice on behalf of women in contentious meetings, as someone out of the spotlight as a supporter but not a leader of a campaigning group. Leo and I continued to live, think, pray, write and work until that way of life was brought to an end by my husband's terminal illness and death. When Leo died in 1987 I was devastated. I had lost my major supporter, my stay, my beloved prayer partner. The doubts increased: the struggle for faith increased. I did not want to go on living.

My husband died when he was 85 years old and when we had been married for thirty years. At the time I thought, and others around me appeared to think, that I should recover from his death in a fairly short time since he had enjoyed an exciting and happy life, both before we met and during our thirty-year marriage. However, within our marriage there were the seeds of pain and bitterness in me because of the treatment that my husband had experienced at the hands of the institutional guardians of Christian morality at the time of our marriage. That punitive treatment returned to my memory when Leo died and threatened to overwhelm me. They were so dreadful that I could not face them. I simply buried my emotional turmoil and it continued to add to my sense of bereavement at a deeper level than my surface consciousness.

I went back to work after a couple of weeks, thinking and believing that that was the best way to help myself to survive. I did wait a year before making decisions about my own future. I thought that was long enough, and became impatient with my passivity. However, with hindsight, I know that I was not ready, even though I thought I was. I made some huge mistakes of judgement during the first three years of widowhood and it took years to untangle myself from decisions I made at the time.

In the first year of bereavement I moved away from my home and went to live in Monmouth, South Wales far from my children, but close to some nuns we had known well during our marriage. I could not bring myself to share my bitterness with the children, and thought to spare them from witnessing my pain. I hoped that by living among those who did believe in God, I could perhaps regain faith as I had once known it. I lived alongside, and then with them, for nearly five years (19). In the second year of bereavement I felt guilty, believing that I had ruined Leo's life by marrying him, so I left my new home and joined the nuns to expiate my sin and try to find faith again. In the third year I went on a thirty-day Ignatian retreat to find out how to live the rest of my life. At the end of the thirty days I knew clearly that I should leave the convent and live alone, but I was too afraid to do so. It was only in the fourth year of bereavement that I got the help I needed from several people including my own doctor, my spiritual director and the convent chaplain. I was then able to take the right path for me. I changed direction, left the convent, sold my house in 1993 and went, as a solitary in life vows, to live in a cottage near the church where I worked as a deacon. I served that church as deacon and priest until 2003.

Had I not made those mistakes and learnt from them, however, I would not have been able to wait wordlessly with other people in their times of despair. It is always possible to force oneself to action: but it may be better to wait for a dynamic energy to emerge in its own time and way.

During these years there were flashes of light from time to time, flashes of intuition that God did exist, and was real. My mind was full of doubts, but those intuitive moments of experience sustained my hopes of a return to faith, as did my extensive reading into the Bible and writers like the Desert Fathers, Julian of Norwich, Nicholas de Cusa, St John of the Cross, and other medieval mystics.

From 1988 onwards I threw myself into the observance of the Anglican faith as a deacon in the Church in Wales and then, from 1997, as a priest. My ordination was an act of sincere though *blind* faith in the existence of God and of solidarity with my sister deacons who that year were allowed to be admitted into the Church in Wales' priesthood (20). All the time I was looking to recover the 'faith of my fathers'. But that did not happen, although I continued to enjoy my pastoral work – that aspect of life closest to my former work as a family doctor – and I knew how to be with people in all kinds of distress and to rejoice with those who could rejoice.

After I was ordained to the priesthood some of the people in our local congregation could not accept that I was a priest and, to our sorrow, left the church where I worked. Others stayed but refused my sacramental ministry. I accepted their strong reactions and most of us managed to live together in the same church community with help from my vicar, the Revd James Coutts, and other clergy and lay supporters. We compromised and enabled most of those who were unable to receive my ministry to remain members of our church. But when Fr James retired I lost a vicar who had been protective of my ministry behind the scenes, and who had given me unobtrusive financial help in expenses and reduced rents of the church property I then occupied. His generosity enabled me to remain active in voluntary ministry using my pension to support myself. It was largely due to him that I was able to do a substantial amount of work with individuals who approached me with moral and relational problems. For it was during this time of early retirement from medicine and with new pastoral responsibilities that some local people and others from much further away began to come to me for spiritual help. I do not know how they found me, but they did: in increasing numbers.

Ruth's story

I would like to share the story of one of the local people I met when I was attached to Monmouth parish as a non-stipendiary assistant deacon. This is a true story and I have Ruth's permission to tell it, but I have disguised certain details to protect her privacy. It reinforces my conviction that some people who come to a devastating 'full stop' in their lives, from which they cannot recover, can sometimes find a totally new way of being that is different and life-giving. No generalisations can be made from this story, for every story is particular to the individuals in them. Its value lies in being able to compare it with our own experiences and help us to see things differently.

Ruth is a person who is representative of many people I have met during my life. She was a young woman in search of love when she reached her maturity as an adult. She had been brought up in a loving home with parents who cherished her, educated her and gave her a good start in her life. As a teenager she fell in love with a young man but, despite parental caution – because the couple came from very different cultures – they married. Ruth left her rural home and went to live in a big city in another part of the country.

Ruth was Christian and her husband was Muslim but they respected one another's viewpoints. They had two children, both girls, who were brought up as Christians. Ruth was happy for several years, but then things went wrong. The secrets of the breakdown of their relationship are known only to them but, in the end, after more than twenty years of marriage, Ruth left her home with her two children. She returned to the area where her parents lived.

After several years alone, Ruth met someone else. This time

she was more cautious about marrying again: but she did. She and Richard, who had also been married before, took the risks and were married at a registry office. They had six years of blissful happiness. Their friends saw Ruth flower through that relationship. Then, while on holiday abroad to celebrate the sixth anniversary of their marriage, Richard died from a heart attack. He had lost consciousness immediately. Ruth had no opportunity to say how much she loved him. She had no time to say goodbye. She found herself alone with his dead body in a country whose language she did not understand, among people she did not know.

At the time of her sudden bereavement Ruth showed courage. Everyone was very kind to her. One of her daughters came to help her make the arrangements but they had to fly home without her husband's body. During all this time she remained calm, rational, and sensible of the need to make practical arrangements for the funeral. She spent much time comforting her children and her parents. She was composed at the funeral. But those of us who knew her well were astonished by her composure. We attributed it to her strong Christian faith and belief in resurrection after death. Two weeks later she returned to work. A couple of weeks afterwards, she rang me up. "I can't go on," she said. "I have come to the end of my strength. I can't think straight. I can't do my work properly. I can't even cry right now. I need help."

Ruth asked to go on sick leave. She did everything to help herself. She talked through the trauma of Richard's death in detail. She did find some comfort in her Christian faith. She sought my help but she returned to work before I thought she was fit to do so. "Ruth is so strong", a mutual friend said to me. "And she has such a rooted faith. She'll be alright."

But she was not alright. Ruth's body broke under the strains imposed on it by the trauma of Richard's unexpected death. Her trauma was increased by other people's expectation that she would manage to get back into her working life within a relatively short span of time. The breakdown in the functioning of her body was complete. She lost her appetite, and in the space of a couple of months she lost ten kilos. She could not sleep or concentrate sufficiently to read. She had no feelings other than periodic bouts of intense grief. For the sake of her now adult children and her elderly parents, she did her best to relate to them whenever she was with them; but all she wanted to do was to crawl away to a quiet corner of her room and lie still. She accepted some medication to help her profound depression, but the pills only took the edge off her pain. She continued to accept counselling help and received it gratefully, yet felt too much like a 'zombie', a living echo of a dead self, to profit by it. Her relatives and friends felt helpless. While she was in this state of numbness she was, they thought, relatively safe. When, however, she would begin to feel again, as she would in time, they feared for her life or sanity. Yet they too felt helpless to offer any remedy other than to try to protect her from unrealistic expectations of a too speedy return to work or any form of 'normal' life.

One day I asked her to try and express her feelings, either through a private diary written to her dead husband, or through abstract painting with colours. I had hesitated to offer this advice. I knew from my own previous experience of bereavement, and from that of waiting for other people to come out of their feelings of numb dislocation, that if grieving people tried activities too early they could regress into an even worse state than before.

Initially, my suggestion seemed to be ignored, but one day – no one knows why she chose that day – Ruth remembered my suggestions. She got out her paints and splashed out some colours in deep swirls: red, orange and yellow. They had no meaning to her at that time, but she quite liked the end result. So she framed it and hung it on her lounge wall above the ledge that held her family photographs. Sometime after that another friend, who did not know Ruth at all well, came to supper when I was

54

visiting. She looked at the abstract picture over the fireplace. "Oh, I like that one," she said. "It has hope in it." Ruth and I looked at the picture. We had not previously seen any hope in it but, sure enough, there was a streak of light paint at the very centre of the picture.

Slowly, over a period of months, other pictures appeared, including a dynamic painting of vibrant blue waves washing over a shore. During all this time Ruth had sometimes been able to vocalise her grief either in her journal, or to her closest friends, but she had not been able to express her feelings in a tangible way. Her speech had sounded flat and factual, emotionless. Through the use of colour and formless swirls she had found a depth of feeling that could at last surface in a new way. Her paintings were a way of her re-entering vitality.

The stories of the people in whom I have seen such profound change taking place motivate me to understand how this discovery of a new way of living comes about. Ruth is someone to whom such a new beginning has happened. The decisive discovery of creative energy within herself altered the direction of her life in a remarkable way. In reflecting on the changes that were brought about through her bereavement, Ruth comments:

When I thought I had found true happiness it was taken away in a split second, but I have been given a depth of under-standing about life and death much more so than before. I have been touched by life and death. This is a gift that has been given to me, against my will. I didn't ask for it, but I have learned to accept it: this is now part of who I am. I can look at the world and see beauty in nature, art, music. When I hear of other people who are going through dreadful times my heart goes out to them, knowing some of their pain from first-hand experience. This is the life-force that unites us in grief and it can be restorative. We are not alone in our grief. We are linked, even united by it. For Christians this is the redemption of Christ on the cross. For non-Christians, it is through the love shown to them by others willing to travel with them and prepared to listen, listen and listen again.

Those who are not Christians may find Ruth's statement about the cross of Christ somewhat bewildering. How can Jesus' suffering an agonising and undeserved death lead to grief being seen as a life giving force? In simple terms Christians see the cross as a victory over the forces of death. For them the love of Jesus towards his enemies and executioners, as well as for his friends, brings them close to Him through the work of the Holy Spirit in their lives. He inspires them and gives them hope that endures and flowers as a beautiful love that can be shared.

Ruth's story has not come to an end. The paintings were but a beginning. Gradually, she was able to think about her future plans: rationally and creatively about what she wanted to do now that she was alone. She was able to make sensible choices and began to alter the direction of her life. She changed her work place, decided to work part time at a relatively easy job whilst, at the same time, developing counselling skills that would lead her into a new profession. She is now a fully qualified professional counsellor who also delights in being a grandmother to two youngsters.

What I have said so far shows the extent to which the grievous suffering caused by coming to a 'full stop' through sudden and unexpected death can interfere with the lives of those who have to live on beyond that death. Ruth's experience could be multiplied many times: death through war and terrorist attack, by suicide and murder, after prolonged unrelieved suffering or by natural and human-made disasters of all kinds. I am talking about extremes of human experience, but such extremes affect everyone's life. Sometimes we feel horror and try to detach ourselves from our feelings. Other times we become overwhelmed by empathic grief, or are provoked to healthy anger and try to prevent a repetition of unnecessary suffering whenever we can. We may become very angry with the people, professions, or governments who cause such suffering with indifference. We may even find ourselves using the idea of 'God' as a focus for our feelings of betrayal by the actions of an implacable force beyond our control: especially when we mourn the death of someone we cherish. We blame God, and then we sometimes lose faith.

Other kinds of bereavement

Ruth's story emphasises the powerful damage that the 'full stop' of physical death can inflict on those who survive bereavements of this kind. But physical death is not the only event that causes people to come to such a stop. Other forms of life-stopping trauma can be just as harmful. Unjust dismissal from employment, imprisonment, involvement in a terrorist attack, becoming a long-term hostage, and paralysing illness can, in a moment of time, be just as destructive. And when life is changed forever in this way, there may be no going back to what was 'before'.

Much has been written about the effects of post-traumatic stress on people's subsequent lives. These accounts inspire those who read them to marvel at the capacity of human beings to recover from such terrible events. I read with awe about people like Terry Waite (21), the survivors of '9/11', and the heroes and heroines of '7/7', since I instinctively feel that I would never be able to recover as they had done. But such people seldom touch our lives as much as those we meet closer to home amongst our friends and neighbours. It has been on those occasions when I have met people like Ruth that I know that I have seen the same kind of heroic transformation among those who would never think of themselves as brave or capable of making such dramatic changes to their ways of life, though often aided by a creative energy that seemingly appeared from nowhere.

The work I did in those Monmouth years began locally but became widespread and was largely unknown in the parish itself. Much of it was with adults who had been sexually abused as children by priests from both Catholic and Anglican Churches. At the time there was a scandal in a neighbouring town where a Catholic paedophile priest was being protected by his bishop. Victims of abuse, clergy accused of this crime, and clergy opposed to the 'coverups' were all coming independently and secretly to talk to me because of my extensive experience in this field. It was confidential and demanding work, but I had the mentoring help of two experts, well-versed in child abuse and the care of adults abused as children. One was a Catholic nun; the other was a Methodist minister.

When Fr James left in 2001 he tried to protect me from those who were opposed to women's ministry in principle. He firmly prevented me from accruing authority and power during the interregnum by planning the services for a whole year. I worked hard under the aegis of the churchwardens, but I also made mistakes in supporting an alternative service that Fr James and I had started for some marginalised people. This service was perceived to be in competition with the main services of the day and so, left without his support, I was vulnerable to criticism. By the time the next vicar arrived, rumour got out that I was well over retiring age and should give way to younger colleagues. Pressure began to build up that I should pay a commercial rent for my home and financially it was becoming more difficult for me to stay around as I had hoped to do.

Yet the Church work had helped me greatly, both to sleep at nights and to feel affirmed by those who happily accepted my ministry. I did not want to retire because work helped my depression so much. My health, however, began to fail. In 2001 I had my left hip replaced for severe arthritis so that I was wheel-chair bound for a time. Then, experiencing terrible chest pain I was wrongly diagnosed as having coronary artery disease only to discover I had a hiatus hernia and oesophageal erosion which had mimicked angina. My ill-health, combined with the fallout from some of my actions during the interregnum and my possibly mistaken suspicion of a putative rent increase, made me accept that I had to retire properly and move my home elsewhere. Consequently in 2003 I moved to Bury in Lancashire to live near to my son Leo.

Chapter 5

Intertwined Lives in Wales

Before I leave the years between 1988 and 2003 I would like to share another story about a family I met after I had retired from active medical practice. This true story describes my struggles to reconcile principles and practice when I was a minister of religion in the Church in Wales. It began when I was a deacon and covers some twenty-six years of my life, as the relationships involved continued after I retired to England. This story has roots in my own youth and development into maturity as a woman and that is why I have chosen it to reflect on how experiences in one generation can still affect people and events in another. In that sense it breaks the narrative sequence of the previous chapters.

Candida's story

Candida's marriage was in serious trouble. Her life story begins with her father, Franklin, who married when he was very young. He had been brought up in a happy and stable home, seemingly untouched by disaster. His expectations of himself as a husband were high. He meant all that he said when he made his marriage vows before God, his family and his friends. He thought Jane shared his views on marriage and he was confident it would last. The marriage appeared to prosper. He worked hard. He had a good profession and he was proud to be able to support his wife. She seemed happy and, in due time, they had four children: two boys and two girls. Franklin ruled the roost. He insisted on tidiness and punctuality. Jane complied at first, but when the children came along she was less submissive inside their home, although outside she was outwardly supportive of all her husband's decisions.

During the first fifteen years of their marriage Franklin and Jane gained a reputation as an ideal middle class, prosperous, professional family. They enjoyed that reputation and sought to preserve it in public. Behind closed doors, however, there were many difficulties over the upbringing of their children. When they had rows the parents kept their counsel. They did not quarrel in front of the children or talk about difficulties outside their own home. In time each adopted secret means of dealing with their children and they responded by adopting different standards of behaviour with each parent. In this way relative peace was sustained within the home. But the family did not realise that the impact of the pervasive tension between the adults was leading to emotional starvation. When the eldest of their children was thirteen years old and the youngest four, tragedy struck without any apparent warning. Franklin came home from work one day to find a note on the hall table: "The children and I have gone. I am not coming back. Do not try and find us." Franklin was frantic. Jane's parents had no idea where she had gone, nor had her neighbourhood acquaintances and friends. The only clue lay in the fact that Jane had taken twenty thousand pounds in cash from their joint account.

Franklin never found out what happened to Jane and their children. His marriage had come to a sudden 'full stop'. He had no idea why she had left him. There was no happy ending, no further contact, or subsequent explanation. She had cut the ties completely. He found no answers to his own unhappiness and was unwilling to find professional help. Each night on the way home from work he got drunk. One night, coming home from the pub, he walked into an oncoming car that had no chance of stopping. His pain was over. But his daughter's was not.

Years later, a long time after Franklin's death, Candida, his youngest child at the time of their departure, decided to try and find out what had happened to her parents' marriage. Alone of the four children, she had grown up with an obsessive nature inherited from her father. Her own marriage to Len had run into difficulties because of her attachment to her work and her refusal to have children, lest she be torn between their needs and her own. She wanted to understand what was happening to her and thereby save her own marriage.

Her search led her to friends who had known Franklin and Jane and who also knew me and that I lived near to Candida. Meeting her at Tymawr convent, I soon realised how disturbed she was by her previous experiences of family break-up and by the apparent failures in her own marriage. I thought that I could offer Candida a supportive relationship that could endure, even though she projected her childhood and marital difficulties on to me. I was, however, blind to some left-over emotional problems of my own that clouded my judgement, even though I was a trained counsellor and had a work mentor to assist me. Consequently we got ourselves into serious difficulties when Candida started to treat me as her own mother. By her own admission, she had then acted in a 'beastly way' towards me to test my patience and love. Sometimes I felt like screaming when she judged my actions to be cruel, when I had sought only to give helpful advice. But I hung on. With my mentor's help our dogged refusal to separate brought us to a deeper understanding of our mutual difficulties.

Later Candida could not easily tell me what had been helpful in this long-term encounter. She simply said she had found herself changing in all sorts of ways that she would not have thought possible when she was younger. Nor can I explain it, but I do know that there was an identifiable point in our relationship when Candida started to listen to *her own emergent wisdom*, rather than to anything I said. From that point on her projections on to me became much less frequent and I gained some insight into my own behaviour towards her. As a result we both started to enjoy our friendship. We still do.

Reflections on Franklin and Candida's stories

The break-up of Franklin and Jane's marriage was due to a funda-mental difficulty in communication. To outsiders they appeared to be compatible yet within their home they never trusted each other sufficiently to speak clearly about their difficulties, particu-larly about their very different attitudes to child rearing. Marriage is dependent on trust, but the inability to communicate honestly with one another can lead to neglect of warning signs. Franklin never noticed his wife's growing discontent and Jane never trusted him enough to confide in him.

This stark tale emphasises that some people who come to a relational 'full stop' do not find their way through the loss of the love they had formerly known for each other. They never reach a creative transformation and so may live the rest of their lives in a kind of shrivelled existence of bitterness and dull grief. Some people, like Franklin, come to the end of their lives unhealed. And Jane's story doesn't necessarily have a 'happy ending' either, for we do not know what happened to her or three of her children.

Candida was more fortunate. Given the freedom of an enduring confidential friendship, she ultimately discovered that many of her marital difficulties had come from her subconscious blame of her mother for taking her away from her beloved father. This had transferred itself into anger towards her husband. She reacted towards him as if he were her mother and behaved in ways that imitated her father's dominating attitudes towards her mother. She found herself deeply conflicted: the tension between the two loves, for her mother and for her father, was threatening her own marriage.

But in time Candida's subconscious hatred of her mother, of which she was quite unaware for many years, gave way to under-standing and compassion. Her defensive love of her father gave way to a more realistic appreciation of his part in the marital breakdown. In the end, she found that she could forgive her parents and let go of her anger and desire for revenge against them. She became more able to separate her childhood relationships from her adult ones. Once she had done that she could develop a new relationship with Len that was free from the damaging effects of the past.

My concept of love

In this story I have spelled out my own experience as a supportive friend and trained counsellor. Too many people carry past mistakes, past wounds and past conditioning into their new relationships. This is what happened to Candida. But it also happened to me.

Attitudes towards love, marriage and relationships have undergone huge changes in the past century. I have told Candida' story exactly as I was told it by her. What I have not yet described is the impact that my experience of the disruption of my own parents' marriage had on my attitudes towards the lives of all those involved in this story. So it seems important to share my own understanding of that very difficult concept 'love' as I have experienced it.

The story I have told about one family reflects British society some fifty years ago and significant changes in moral values have happened since then. I was born in 1925, Candida some thirty years later. The values I grew up with are not, generally speaking, universally acknowledged in today's Britain and my concept of love may be dated as it's rooted in a time when our culture was Christian and the Church of England had an important role in society. Consequently I am speaking of 'love' as a commitment to a *married* relationship: "for better or worse," as the 1662 Book of Common Prayer puts it, "for richer or poorer, in sickness and in health, until death do us part." People of my age will have heard these words many times. They describe an expectation that people were familiar with and wanted to observe. And even though its impact on families – especially on the children trapped in unhappy homes – was sometimes damaging to all concerned, it did nonetheless hold many people together when their marriage was under considerable strain.

That was how I was brought up to think of a successful marriage, though my own life was very different. I adored my mother. I wanted her to be happy. I spent at least eleven years of my childhood longing for my parents' reunion, but when I finally realised that this was not going to happen I too shared her bitterness at our plight. At school I hated being without a father when so many other children had apparently happy families. Divorce was a terrible disgrace. I lied to my friends by pretending that he had died in a plane crash. When I was found out, I was sternly rebuked, made to tell the truth, and hated my father even more. In all those years I only met with him twice. When aged nineteen I became an Anglican; I was encouraged to find ways of forgiving my father without being disloyal to my mother. Reluctantly I began to meet with him a little more often, but it was only when my mother was dying that I felt any warmth towards him because he visited her during the last few days of her life and was tender towards her. After she died I felt freer to get to know him and to take his grandchildren to see him. We gradually found a way of enjoying our relationship and I was able to understand his point of view rather better than I had done.

Yet I remained an absolutist about the indissolubility of Christian marriage (22). I had strict views about the sanctity and indissolubility of my own marriage and tended to be judgemental about other people's inability to endure difficulties in their marriages. It was only when I became a family doctor with four young children of my own that I began to encounter people like Franklin and his daughter, Candida. By that time I had discovered compassion, born out of my own failures as wife and mother; then I began to see love, especially marital love, in a rather different and very much less judgemental light.

'Love' is a difficult word to unpack, particularly today when society is so fractured that concepts like fidelity, commitment, and the permanence of a relationship do not seem to have meaning for many people, and where children may grow up in many different circumstances. But this difficulty affects all of us. For how do we know that commitment to a relationship is a sign of love? It might be a sign of stubbornness or a particularly cruel form of revenge. It might be a sign of dogged duty without the balm of emotional love. So my definition of 'love' immediately calls for a qualification: that love *always desires the best outcome for the loved one*. But what *is* the best outcome?

As a practising Anglican during the years of my medical practice I gradually changed my attitude from an absolutist stance to a more relativist view. It was one thing to adhere to my own marriage vows in an absolutist way but it was a very different matter to expect people to agree with my understanding (23). My medical knowledge, experience, and compassion eventually came together after I was ordained, and many came to share their own stories and responses to marital difficulties with me with an openness that still astonishes me.

Today there is no consensus on what love is. Each of us has to work out our own philosophy of life. Even if we adopt the 'official' line of the Church, we will inevitably come upon many different views about the way our intimate relationships should be lived. Yet marriage and stable relationships remain precious to many individuals and many do long for happiness and permanence in their lives. But they don't necessarily have the resources to overcome the difficulties inherent in all long-term relationships.

Anita's story

There is another story that comes out of these Monmouth years, one that I find salutary because it reveals the difficulties I had as an inexperienced priest who thought she had dealt with her own childhood problems through her psychiatric training. I had not, and this threatened to undermine my therapeutic relationship with Anita.

Anita's relationship with me began in Monmouth and it has continued to this day. It was while I was living as an 'alongsider' at the convent, and not as a member of the community, that I met her. Maybe it is easier to pour our heart out to a complete stranger? I don't know, but Anita did find it possible to confide in me. Hers is a story about human trust in other people and in human institutions.

Trust is a foundation gift of human birth. We are born helpless and totally dependent and the first people we trust are those who care for us during infancy. As we develop and our world expands we continue to take things on trust. We believe what we are told by those we trust: whether it's the story of Father Christmas or those occasions when, visiting the doctor, we are told that a treatment 'won't hurt'; or that a parent will return 'soon', even when we suspect they will be gone for some time. Most of us get used to this kind of loss of trust in others and we learn not to transfer our experience to *all* people. But when adults repeat the occasions that cause mistrust often enough, and about more serious matters, some children become suspicious of all so-called 'truths' from parents or authority figures. And inability to trust is a serious handicap to our well-being. This is was what happened to Anita.

Anita knew that her father loved her. She knew it from his words to her and from his gestures of affection. In part this was because he talked to her a lot, explained things to her, and helped her to feel utterly safe in his company. So it was a terrible shock when he took her to the doctor for an immunisation and told her it would not hurt. Worse than that, he had left her alone with a nurse who pinned her down for the injection. She felt terrified and violated but she said nothing to her father. This was the first time she had known an adult to lie to her and, although she went on loving her father, she no longer trusted him or other adults.

Family life at home was not happy. Anita's parents shouted at one another and came to blows. She was torn between her love for her mother and for her father, and in her own way she tried to make peace between them. But when she was only thirteen years old, her father died.

Her mother was left to bring up the children on her own. Her personality seemed to have changed, especially in regard to her eldest daughter's behaviour. Anita was expected to set a good example to her younger brothers and sisters. She also got punished more than them. Her mother's anger frightened her and made her feel unloved. Deep inside herself, the child knew that she loved her mother more than she could say: she constantly tried to please her. But her attempts did not seem to work. Had she been a less sensitive child she might have avoided being damaged but, as the years passed, her fear of punishment – especially from women in authority over her – became ingrained. Her small mistakes and naughtiness became a source of self-condemnation.

Anita was a clever child but she did not do well at school, being too shy and afraid of criticism to risk putting her ideas to the test by revealing her own opinions. She undervalued her own intelligence, ability and considerable gifts. She also developed a habit of blaming herself for anything that went wrong at home or at school. When her mother became unhappy, Anita blamed herself. When one of the other children became ill, she felt guilty; she tried her hardest to be good and to do anything that would please her mother.

Anita's sense of being responsible for all that went wrong in her family and school was misplaced, but it persisted into her adult life. The eventual outcome of this gradual sustained loss of trust in her own wisdom and gifts was that, in adult life, she tended to compare herself unfavourably with her peers. She accepted blame for events that were not her fault. And this proved to be a serious handicap in her relationships in subsequent places of employment. Her employers and peers found themselves irritated when she persisted in saying 'sorry' for other people's shortcomings. She found herself becoming the habitual office scapegoat and, when this happened, she would 'move on' to another job. It became a pattern in her life. She hated it. Then one day she came to a 'full stop' and had a complete breakdown in her health. This did not help Anita's self-confidence at all; nor did reassurance that she could be helped back to full health. She was convinced that 'it was all her fault'. She became depressed. Friends and colleagues found it difficult to understand what had happened because previously she had seemed to be a strong person, always ready to listen to their troubles, always steady in moments of crisis. When they came to visit her in hospital they could not believe that the weepy and subdued person they encountered was Anita.

After a while Anita recovered enough to leave hospital, but she was now dependent on pills to help her anxiety. This didn't help either, for she hated the pills and continually tried to reduce the dose or stop them altogether. When she did, she relapsed. The first time she went on to long-term invalidity benefit she cried. The next time, she said nothing. The time after that, she lost hope of being able to work again. She had lost trust in her ability to recover. She had tried all sorts of talking therapies as well but they didn't seem to help. She had lost trust in herself and in her own worth as a human being. She retired early on grounds of ill health, feeling herself to be a failure. She moved home and, happily, came to an area with excellent psychiatric services, where she was able to have effective medication and prolonged counselling and support. Anita's story illustrates the tragedy that can befall anyone who temporarily loses trust and becomes sensitised to fear through that loss. Happily Anita is now on the way to a fuller and happier life. She has even begun to love herself, 'warts and all', as God loves her: something she did not know before her illness.

Chapter 6

Retirement in England

I do not regret any of the years I spent in Wales. Both Tymawr convent and Monmouth parish taught me a lot that has stood me in good stead. But in 2003 I moved away from Wales and came to live in England near one of my children. I was still an observant Anglican woman priest at that time. The move was a seismic event because I left a close Christian community as well as a role as a working assistant priest in a busy parish. I moved to Bury in Lancashire, an area I did not know and became a retired priest in the diocese of Manchester.

Initially I missed the Christian friends I had in Monmouth more than I could say. Some have kept in regular touch, while others have continued to offer me hospitality and friendship when I return on brief visits. But I had to begin again in a new environment, one which knew little about my previous life and work. Soon after my arrival I found an Anglican parish on the internet that looked friendly towards the idea of women priests and began to attend. I enjoyed it and was accepted as a retired priest by the then vicar, Fr Ian Stamp, and his large team of non-stipendiary clergy and potential ordinands. The churchmanship was very different from that in Monmouth. There was no daily Eucharist and no daily Matins and Evensong. And Sunday worship was much less formal than I was used to, but the more Anglo-Catholic churches in my immediate area were unable to welcome the sacramental ministry of women priests.

However, during my first year there I found that I missed the regular daily rhythm of Mass, Matins and Evensong. I felt lost without that rhythm and my prayer life began to suffer. A Catholic friend of mine, Irene, saw that I was feeling unhappy and she took me to our then local Catholic priest, Fr Rob

Morrow, who allowed me to go to his church on the days when there was no Anglican Eucharist that I could get to.

Fr Morrow was an Irish priest with a very loving heart. I went to Mass at his church on Mondays, Tuesdays, Fridays and Saturdays until his retirement in 2008. On Sundays, other weekdays and Feast days I went to my Anglican Church. This was in the days when the Bible readings and texts of the Eucharistic services were very similar because both denominations used the ICEL texts in their liturgies (24). I felt at home in both churches and, after a while, I was able to receive Holy Communion in the Catholic Church because I fulfilled the conditions for a worshipper who could not worship in her own church but believed all the core beliefs of Catholics, even though she belonged to a different denomination. There were many Anglo-Catholics like me at the time, though probably few as plagued by doubt as I was.

Fr Ian Stamp, my Anglican vicar, was a great delegator and a friend of Fr Morrow. He knew what I was doing. I also began to get involved in ecumenical relationships with the Catholic Parish and in interfaith relations with our local Sufi mosque. I worked with, Fr Morrow, one of our Anglican suffragan bishops, Rt Revd David Gillett, and another priest the Revd Keith Trivasse and his priest wife Margaret to promote harmonious interfaith relations in our area. I found this work stimulating and enriching to my understanding of prayer and worship in different faiths but the doubts persisted.

Trying to remain a practising Christian in this new environment meant that I had to struggle on without as much support as I had become accustomed to in Wales. I did so uneasily, but it became apparent to me that my intellectual doubts about some of the doctrines of the Church were getting stronger and stronger. I felt paralysed by disbelief, yet unwilling to acknowledge it publicly, or to relinquish my public role. However, through all this time I was still able to say 'Jesus is

Lord' – even without fully understanding what I meant by that phrase – and so felt able to continue to be an active retired priest.

During this time my work with individuals in relational difficulties continued. People just kept turning up. One of these was Petra.

Petra's story

Petra was not a professional violinist, but she came from a musical family and she grew up loving her violin. The emotional demands of her professional role weighed on her mind and music was a constant source of joy and helped her to relax after a heavy day's duty as a social worker in a deprived area of a large city. One evening she stepped into her garden to enjoy the scent of the early jasmine and slipped and fell. Petra knew she had hurt her elbow badly, but at the time she made light of her injury. She went to her local hospital and, collared and cuffed, supplied with ample pain killers and an appointment for a return visit, she went home. It was not until some weeks later that she began to realise that her stiff elbow was not mending in the way she had expected. And it was over a year before she accepted that she would not play the violin again. That particular hope had come to a 'full stop'.

Her disability was a profound disappointment and affected her emotional mood. She slipped into a gradually increasing state of depression. Her malaise and apathy affected her work to such an extent that she needed help. She came to me for soul friendship (25). I was sympathetic. I tried to make all sorts of suggestions to replace her music with another form of artistic expression such as painting but, to my amazement, this suggestion was greeted with fury: "I've no ability to imagine what a room I want to decorate might look like," she said. "I've no talent for colour!" She became tearful. I recognised there was more to the outburst than I had at first realised. Knowing that anger and fear are sometimes linked and that we push frightening events into the deepest recesses of our minds and repress them from consciousness, I gently invited Petra to think of any occasion when she had experienced great fear. In time she was able to recall one incident when she had been shut into a dark cupboard as a punishment and her imagination had run riot. Recalling this, Petra trembled and sweated, re-enacting her terror at finding the cupboard door locked. I refrained from further suggestions and waited.

Some months later, and partly recovered from her loss of hope about her injury, Petra was watching her friend Lucy making a beautiful collage and suddenly experienced a desire to do the same. It might, she thought, help some of the children she frequently met in the course of her work to express their feelings. She began to allow her hands to play with the different materials and, without thinking she began to put items on to a sheet of paper. Only then, did she discover their meaning as they sprang to life in a quite new way: and she was astonished by what she was seeing.

Change did not come overnight and Lucy's encouragement had a lot to do with it. The imaginative part of Petra's brain that had been dormant for so long began to flourish. Collage play, and other forms of abstract art became natural to her and were also taken up eagerly by some of the children she cared for. Symbols of love in the form of a series of warm rose-coloured hearts began to appear in many of Petra's collages. The children picked this up and began to express their feelings in the same way. Petra's art was easy to understand but quite complex affective themes could find expression through very simple illustrations and everyday symbols.

Petra's accident dislocated her life. But eventually it also exposed the reason for her apparent inability to use her imagination when she was able to recapture the original horror of her imprisonment and the suffocating feeling that she had buried for so long. Her long subconscious repression of the memory had protected her from situations in which she had to imagine a domestic environment in which there were cupboards that represented for her the death of hope. And the recall of this despair provoked the outburst that led her to the truth.

Petra's story shows how one event in childhood can dislocate a person's life and lead to an impoverishment of her ability to make imaginative leaps at all. "I can't imagine what it might be like," became a kind of watchword that made her believe she had virtually no capacity for visual imagination. She had lost hope in her ability to use her energies creatively. She knew that certain 'trigger' events could send her into a complete panic and for many years she did her best to avoid anything that made her feel 'shut in' or trapped in a situation without any apparent hope of escape. The resolution of Petra's predicament was, I believe, only made possible after she received professional help in regard to the original trauma. That enabled her to discover a latent talent with the help of her artist friend Lucy. She had found the freedom to hope, but in a different way. The experience was transformative, not only for her, but for those for whom she cared.

My inability to conform to expectations

Petra's friendship with me began to undermine my doubts about the existence of God because the change in her was so transformative that I began to hope that I was seeing the Holy Spirit at work. The change in my friend convinced me that my doubts might also one day yield to faith; but my difficulties with the institutional Church remained.

My first five years in Bury passed happily. I had found a *modus vivendi* that helped me to live as a solitary, accountable for her life vows to an Anglican bishop. I was, however, still troubled by some of the Anglican teaching that had been promulgated at the Lambeth Conference of 1998 (26) and was then reinforced in that of 2008 (27). I was still working to support women priests who were encountering discrimination because of their gender, still hoping to see experienced senior women priests in the Church of England be allowed to become bishops in that Church (as they had been in some of the other Churches in the Anglican Communion) and I was still trying to do what I could to support gay, lesbian and transgender priests throughout the world, some of whom were suffering even more greatly in countries other than our own.

It was in this state of mind that I went to the 2008 Lambeth Conference of Anglican bishops to petition their Lordships to adopt more inclusive attitudes towards women and homosexuals. Going to Lambeth, not as an 'insider' but as a supporter of disadvantaged women and gay, lesbian and trans-gender people, meant that I was openly opposed to some of the discriminatory practices of the Church of England towards these people. I now found myself unable to subscribe to what the hierarchy of the Church wanted me to conform to in practice. Most of the Lambeth Fathers did not appear to agree with those of us who supported the spiritual leadership of women, or of men and women in stable homosexual partnerships. The previous Lambeth Conference in 1998 had been opposed to our beliefs about human nature and now, ten years later, had formally reiterated their majority view. Lambeth 2008 continued its appeal for a world-wide moratorium on the consecration of actively homosexual men as bishops and there was still hesitation about the ordination and consecration of women as priests and bishops within the Anglican Communion even though, by that time, some women had been legally consecrated bishops in some Anglican provinces. One active homosexual priest, the Revd Gene Robinson, had become a bishop in the Episcopal Church in America in 2003 and this particular action polarised opinion throughout the Anglican Communion (28).

This disappointment was the starting place for a more extensive review of my own beliefs in some of the other doctrinal issues of my Anglican faith, particularly in relation to notions of universal salvation. I could no longer believe that people had to be Christians to enter into God's kingdom. A few weeks later I realised that I could no longer conform to what was expected of me as an active priest of the Anglican Communion. I had reached a crisis point over my difficulties with faith as taught by a majority of the Lambeth bishops. I asked to stop exercising a public priestly ministry in the Church of England. My request was accepted by my diocesan bishop.

Chapter 7

A Major Crisis of Conscience

The Lambeth Conference of 2008 marked a moment of major crisis in my life. It was not, however, the Lambeth Conference alone that had brought about my resignation from public priestly ministry, though it might have been the 'straw that broke the camel's back'. More important contributions to my crisis of conscience came from the friends who had once been my companions in campaigning for changes towards women and homosexuals, but who had now left the Church altogether. Their arguments with me about their departure from the institutional Church were most disturbing to my own faith. One of these friends, Irene, represents a number of people whose own doubts provoked even more doubts in me.

Irene's story

Irene had originally visited me in Wales in search of a new soul friend, having converted to Catholicism as a young student of philosophy. She was also well acquainted with research into brain functions and, after university, had become interested in the mystics and how some descriptions of mystical experiences could be related to brain functioning. I suppose that the fact that I was both a medical doctor and a practising Christian helped her to feel that I might understand her own journey. Our friendship continued when I moved to Bury and it was she who encouraged me to visit Fr Morrow.

We had some great times Irene and I during the initial years of our friendship. I learnt a great deal about Catholic spirituality and about the Spanish mystics. We shared an ability to see meaning through abstract images and symbolic acts, and gained insights into ways in which truth could be conveyed in nonverbal communication. We shared some mutual doubts about our respective churches in regard to some of the disciplines that conflicted with our core beliefs in attitudes towards creation and scientific insights into human nature. She thought my religion was too easy-going and tolerant. I thought hers was too authoritarian, centralised in its governance, and harsh towards those whom it deemed disobedient.

At the time when we met I was still struggling with doubt and disbelief, but was fiercely clinging to my allegiance to the Anglican Church as one of its deacons. So when, a few years later, she told me that she thought she no longer believed in the existence of God, I was both surprised and upset. I thought I would have to stop talking with her about spiritual things, about those mysterious 'realities' that appeared to lie in the spaces between spoken words, the nuances of relationships, and the strange activity of prayer; for I had always supposed that concepts like truth, beauty and goodness were concepts that depended upon absolute faith in God.

How wrong I was about Irene! Taking God out of the equation made no difference at all to us. She found the numinous in beauty. I found 'God' in beauty. It became obvious to me that we were talking about an experience that we could not quantify other than as mystery (29). The difference between us was in the way we responded to the loss of trust in the institution we had originally trusted too readily. Irene's trust in the teaching authority of her church had been undermined. Her doubts had solidified, yet she still felt that she could live with mystery, which she attributed to her human nature. I had designated that mystery as 'God' but had added a whole lot of pre-requisites gained from my theological studies. I had plenty of doubts, but subsumed them into obedient compliance to the creeds and church teaching. Neither of us could prove to the other that we were right: but the authority for our faith was also ours in the long run. And my faith in the life-force that I had named God remained as strong as ever, despite my loss of trust in the church as a source of truth.

'Letting go, and letting God'

When Irene lost her trust in her church's authority and in the existence of God, she seemed to be unconcerned. "I can live without institutional faith," she said, "as so many other people have also found." But I was the one who was most disturbed by Irene's declaration and, consequently, my own compliance to prevalent church teaching came under scrutiny. In large part I believe this was due to my condition at the time, for I was still clinging in 'blind trust' to the beliefs propounded by the Church of England.

Such doubts about faith are common among religious people who, if they have the courage to do so, will sometimes allow themselves to see their faith through the eyes of sceptics and realise how the 'insider' language of faith, formerly common-place, now seems like 'mumbo jumbo' to many: making them perhaps feel obliged to restrict their religious faith to a private part of their lives. For some like Irene, their doubts may indeed cause the death of trust in the institutional church and even of their faith in the existence of God. However, what Irene taught me is that the 'full stop' that comes as loss of trust in, and compliance with, the church's authority may actually be an event that leads us towards *new* adventures, *new* ways of living, *new* joys and, indeed, *new* forms of trust. For, though one form of trust may have died, another form – perhaps altogether more mysterious – may replace it.

At this stage of my life it seems to me that this call to 'let go into mystery' is an invitation to explore the nature of creation and our role within it; and our inability to provide satisfactory answers to our questions and doubts is a positive help in shaping the value systems we embrace and the way we live. (Providing, of course, that we don't expect everyone else to adopt the same value system, or judge others for choosing different values.) I think the loss of trust I have been exploring is a doorway into pivotal changes in attitude that can lead to a greater partnership between human beings, and between humanity and the social and natural environments with which we are intimately connected.

My own journey between 1980 and 2008, years of profound doubt and darkness, did not end either in atheism or in the recovery of the literal belief in the Creeds that I formerly held with integrity. During these years of dark confusion when I wandered through many deserts with a profound sense of the absénce of God, I did not recognise that I was being accompanied in my search for truth by a dynamic creative Energy because I could not, despite occasional glimpses, fully perceive that darkness *might* embody such Energy; even though this was precisely what was sustaining me in my wandering! So not until 2008 would I admit to myself that I could no longer teach, preach or exercise any official clerical ministry in the Church of England even though I can now affirm that I loved being a minister of the Church during the years when I was a deaconess, a deacon and finally a priest in the Anglican Communion. Instead I continued to cling to the joy I had aspired to during so many years of dogged endeavour to enable women to be admitted to the threefold ordained ministry of that Church.

It was, I think, only when I admitted the reality of my loss of faith as I once knew it, that I began to be reborn: though I have to say that the beginnings of this new life were more like my idea of purgatory than resurrection life! For many months I still wandered about in a kind of dark doubt, both in my condition and in my life as a woman who still frequented prayer, Bible reading and church attendance. Yet there had been a change; for though I felt that I wanted to deny the existence of God and just 'get on with my life,' I could not do so. And while I was no longer searching for a recovery of compliant belief, I *was* looking for Life and Love in new ways.

Discovering Unconditional Love

The Anglican Church I belonged to preached about God's 'unconditional love'; yet in practice its members often appeared to exhibit a love that was conditional on 'good behaviour'. This did not mean that Unconditional Love didn't exist, for love outpoured in Creative Energy does exist. Unconditional Creative Love – a term which for me encompasses the doctrine of the Trinity – is personified in the incarnate person of Jesus. He faced evil, lived with it, and managed to overcome it in all sorts of ways. The legacy of His life, death and resurrection is expressed through the person of the Holy Spirit who continues to teach us to live fully human lives and so to 'glorify God' (Gal 2:20). This insight into the nature of Love and the outpouring of Energy within creation had gradually opened my eyes to my *own* fragility in attempting to reveal Love towards friends and enemies alike. After my long journey through faith, and honed by doubt, I had found a mode of belief I felt I could own.

This was the first insight that led to a change in my negatively critical attitude towards the institutional Church. The truth was that I could still find signs of Unconditional Love at work there. The love shown by my companion Christians, although not unconditional, pointed towards Love itself. I found the expression of Love alive in creation and I even found it in myself. I found it too in the little people of faith who were despised by most Christians as 'unorthodox' or 'downright sinners'. I found it in people who were atheists. And I found it in some of my fellow Christians who had set their faces against the principle of women's full partnership with men in the Church, and who were against active homosexuality. Once I let go of the notion that the Church had to behave as a perfect Body and accepted that human love could, and did, point to a greater Love rather than to its own poor example, I received another insight; namely that, though my ideals and ideas were also flawed by my humanity, I too could point to Love without insisting that my views were right and everyone else's were wrong.

In living among oppressed people, I had also discovered the truth that the oppressed are also people who don't always treat their 'enemies' with the respect or love they deserve as fellow human beings. On both 'sides' there are different interpretations of Scripture, different theological views and understandings of orthodoxy. And we all experience self-hatred and fear of difference that may make us act in destructive ways towards our fellow humans. We all have within ourselves a complexity of beliefs, emotions, experiences and prejudices that influence our behaviour. And this realisation changed me from a campaigner into a seeker for reconciliation and partnership with those with whom I profoundly disagreed.

This change was not the result of a sudden revelation, but the fruit of years of struggle during which I had begun to grow in understanding of those to whom I was opposed in matters of personal conscience. It took years to effect this change: for such change takes place at a deeper level than intellectual belief, deeper even than feelings and experience. These years of doubt and pain had born fruit and brought me to the point of action. It was as if a veil had been lifted from my eyes so that I was able to see God indwelling creation, continually encouraging us to see Love at work by using our own capacity for love to help us to grow towards the source of Love itself (Rom 8:22-30).

This loss of compliance with the theological reasoning of Lambeth 2008 led, however, to something I had never known before. I recognised that I was so changed that I could no longer observe the proprieties of behaviour as a Christian member of a single denomination. I could no longer see denominational prescriptions of acceptable behaviour as useful or be loyal to one Christian denomination. This discovery appalled me. And I needed to challenge it in some way.

I longed for a transformation in my attitudes towards faith and I began to search for the Energy of Creative Love and so a faith that I could believe and live with integrity. Some people did at the time comment that I was a wandering seeker, rootless and always moving on: yet, to me it felt as if my roots were, in fact, going deeper in search of that elixir of Life and Love and of a way to live in its strength. I realised that the 'feeling' that God existed would not come back in the way I longed for it to return, but I was no longer paralysed by my disbelief. I was on a journey again. I did not know where I was going: except that I was in the company of a mystery I could not identify or comprehend. That mystery had opened my eyes to the presence of the dance of love at work in all creation, and to the discovery that I was part of that dance.

The Creeds of my Christian faith no longer mattered as they had once done. They were no longer vital to my belief in what I could now call faith in the Energy of Unconditional Love. This phrase 'Unconditional Love' had distillated the idea of God for me. My doubts had been dissipated by the strong conviction about the existence of a creative Energy that I could think of as God, the 'ground of all being' as Paul Tillich had described it (30). What had begun to matter far more than the doubts that plagued my mind was a deep-rooted belief in, and experience of, a living Energy within each present moment; an Energy I identified with its origins in Love.

The unexpected result of my 'new birth'

This discovery was both exhilarating and frightening: but the journey was not over. When I separated myself from the official duties of an ordained member of the Anglican Communion, and asked to be taken off the list of 'approved clergy' with the bishop's Permission to Officiate in the diocese, I was of course questioned as to why I wanted to take that step: and I was also challenged.

Some of my friends assumed I was angry with the Church of England. I was; but in previous years that anger would not have led to resignation but, rather, to deeper engagement in an effort to secure further change. Some thought that I was opting out of my interior conflict by laying down my active functions as a priest and retiring into a graceful old age. But that was not how I saw it. I simply thought that if I was to try to live as a human being seeking Unconditional Creative Love, I could not go on behaving as if there was a 'them and us': whereby my opinions expressed the truth and no one else's did. I could not go on proclaiming my belief in a resurrection life that was unavailable to people who were not people of religious faith or that – according to some of my Christian neighbours – was unavailable to anyone who did not share their particular beliefs. I could not go on belonging to a public ministry that demanded I proclaim beliefs I no longer held. Instead, I acted in a manner that I could not fully understand, but that I felt in my bones was a 'call' from God.

With hindsight now I admit that at the time I did not trust my own ability to renounce the practice of my priesthood if I remained an Anglican. I thought I might 'cave in' if I stayed an Anglican. And, since I believe that God may use fear creatively for good at certain times in our lives, it is this very fear itself that may have contributed to my conversion to Catholicism.

Having found Unconditional Creative Love – God – in the oppressed people of the world, I knew it must also be found in those who oppressed others in the belief that they were right to do so. Consequently I set myself to find that Love within that most autocratic of institutions: the Catholic Church. This move felt to me like the ultimate test in my quest for Love in places that were not immediately attractive to me, since many of the features of Catholicism go against the grain of my own opinions.

"A perverse decision?"

On hearing that I had joined the Catholic Church, one of my former Anglican priest colleagues called it 'a perverse decision'. I agreed with him. After all, I had always said I would *never* join the Catholic Church because of its hierarchical structures, its system of governance that excluded most laity from decision making and its attitude towards women and homosexuals.

When I went for a short retreat to a Cistercian monastery in the autumn of 2008 I was of the same mind. I had already decided to leave active ministry in the Church of England and I expected this move would take me into quiet retirement or even into a rest from organised institutional religious observance. I did not know what to do next. That was why I had taken time off to think. While at the monastery I spent some time alone in the large austere church and, one day, I encountered a vibrant Energy there that overwhelmed me. It turned my life upside down, for I felt it was driving me to continue my search within the ranks of the Catholic Church. It seemed impossible but, with Unconditional Love manifested in amazing Energy, 'nothing is impossible'.

I waited for several weeks after this unexpected encounter, thinking myself to be deluded. It seemed so 'out of character', so contrary to all that I had stood for and done within the Anglican Church that I loved so deeply. Nor did I did want to betray my women priest colleagues. Moreover, if I could not conform to the doctrines of the Church of England I certainly could not conform to what might be expected of a Catholic convert.

Gradually, I came to understand that my entrance into the Catholic Church was unreasonable to nearly everyone who knew me well; and it was certainly inexplicable to me. My conversion was based on intuition about the nature of Unconditional Love. For Unconditional Love has no logic. It sometimes demands the sacrifice of the most precious gifts given by the Creative Energy I call God: in my case the public exercise of my Anglican priesthood. I had no idea why I should take such a step. I just did; and I was fortunate in finding a Catholic priest who accepted the sincerity and validity of my desire for conversion and instruction.

It is only now, some six years after my reception into the Catholic Church that I can begin to understand how essential that step was for me. As a long-time explorer of contemplative prayer I had gradually been led to a place where those who live lives of prayer encounter the egotism and evils that dwell in the depths of their own being. Like the fourth-century hermits and the medieval anchorites and anchoresses, I had eventually fled into a solitary way of life to struggle with my own evil and "against the cosmic powers of this present darkness, against the spiritual forces of evil in the heavenly places (Eph 6:12)." But it was a solitude partly of my own making, and it was not until I came to be 'enclosed' in the Catholic Church – making it impossible for me to carry out the public ministry of a woman priest in the Church of England – that I understood that confinement within this anchorage not of my own making *could* ultimately lead to freedom.

This new understanding of the reality of the existence of Unconditional Love, and its manifestation within creation itself, involved a radical change in my way of life. It meant surrender to the unknown. It meant agnosticism in the full sense of that word: being able to live in the 'present moment' and finding 'eternal life' there, without the assurance of knowing that there was a personal resurrection life after death. It meant that my faith was not reliant on adherence to doctrine, so much as on a personal experience of that Unconditional Creative Love.

This is a difficult concept to understand, but I believe that some revelation of it is present at some stage in many people's lives, although many do not often talk openly about such changes in perception and belief as they grow older. I am trying to describe how this discovery of a new form of faith affects people to whom it happens, irrespective of how it happens. I do not feel that I had any part in prompting my own encounters with Creative Love – other than my determination to seek it – for I believe that what I am describing comes as a gift from that Love itself.

The fruits of encountering Unconditional Creative Love

This story has not been easy to write. The mystery I have described in my own life is the mystery of life itself, the mystery of the changes that take place within a person's life even though she retains the same unique identity. Her identity is represented by a personal name, to which she continues to respond; yet she is always becoming a new creature. This change may take place suddenly or gradually. It may be adaptive or reactive to outside situations. It is mirrored in the natural rhythms of life and death and in the company of all creation. Every meeting with any kind of 'other' – animate or inanimate – contributes to the metamorphosis that is taking place, without the individual necessarily being aware that anything is happening. These changes are, I believe, *part* of the evolution of God's cosmos (Jn 1:1-18); but my personal belief is that some of these changes happened because I had been touched by Creative Love at various points in my life, and that it was more than evolution: it was grace (31).

When people have been touched repeatedly and in ever deeper ways by Unconditional Love, some of them – whatever their level of belief – do seem to exhibit certain changes in their previous thinking and behaviour that are directly linked to this experience. One mark is that a person finds it possible to love *all* their neighbours, not just those who agree with them or are likeable. This doesn't require a person to like being persecuted or oppressed, or not to feel hatred. But it means that the person resolves not to answer hate with hate, cruelty with cruelty, or death with revenge. We see that mark in the lives of many Christian martyrs and selfless people, but we also see it in non-

Christians.

Another mark is that a person becomes unable to judge others in respect of their moral values. This is the great mystery underlying the actions of those who find it possible to forgive horrendous actions from other human beings – even those who have killed or maimed their relatives, those who have unjustly imprisoned them, or those who deny others their basic human rights. It is the great mystery that underlies the actions of people who are, or become, non-judgemental in their attitudes towards sinners, though not towards the evil acts that they commit.

But perhaps the most important mark is that one who is so touched becomes content to be able to say 'I do not know'. I do not know if Jesus Christ was born without a human father. I do not know how His resurrection took place in bodily terms but I do see the results of the disciples' encounters with that Love through observing the changes in their former behaviour, and through seeing evidence of Love incarnate in Jesus Christ. I do not know if there is a resurrection life after death, but I can trust in actions that I see to be close to God's idea of Love incarnate. I may say 'yes' by faith to all these questions, and I have done. Indeed, I continue to be a practising institutional Christian: but I know that I do not know. I will only find out when I die. Meantime I am content to be a prisoner of hope, a willing person who trusts what they do not know to be there – but who acts on that belief.

The interconnectedness of creation

I have started my new adventure into an unknown and, I would say, unknowable future by doing the unthinkable; or at least what I had formerly thought I could never do. I did not stop being a Christian or proclaim myself to be an atheist, but I remain instead a Christian who is content *not* to know the answers to mystery. I am a Christian within my own understanding of incarnate Love. For my desire is to follow the Way of Creative Love and I have discovered that the way I am called to do this is to cross all sorts of boundaries which I believe have been made by human beings who have not yet discovered the full meaning of the Love that is content to 'descend into hell'.

I am trying to learn to live in the 'present moment' and to find Love there. All I do know – and it is a discovery shared by many who have let go of any adherence to the institutional faith they once clung to – is that I remain a 'prisoner of hope': a "hope that does not disappoint us, because God's Love has been poured into us through the Holy Spirit that has been given to us (Rom 5:5)." And this hope leads us to encounter the energy of Love wherever it may be found in creation.

This profound awareness of the interconnectedness of all creation comes most easily to those who have an intense desire to find space for an emptiness that can embrace silence, and those who can resist busyness in all its seductive forms. All the major religions encourage their adherents to seek this space for emptiness and reflection. Yet they also make it very difficult for people to avoid feeling guilty about taking the time and energy that is necessary to develop such awareness. Those who do choose to pursue contemplative prayer are sometimes expected to feel guilty about the changes in their lives and beliefs that take place subsequently.

I do not feel guilty at all; change is part of the human condition, part of growth, part of the purpose of life itself. I have written about my own journey, because I am the only person I know who can give permission for such an honest account. There are always consequences after self-exposure of any kind, but I am too old now for it to matter. Yet, I consider that the authorised representatives of the Churches whom I know best, and still love, have lost their ability to be honest in this way. So perhaps it is for individuals near the end of their lives to speak out about dogmas and beliefs produced in the past that now seem absurd and need to be revised. For it appears to me that some church leaders I have known, loved and served all my life, are pre-occupied with issues that *do not matter* at all to most church members. So maybe the renaissance of faith in our own age will come from those ordinary people without power or status who are subject to institutional religious hierarchies: and from the questions they ask.

Facing hard questions

Such honesty raises hard questions, not least about the mystery that is God which I understand to be a dynamic cosmic Energy found within creation itself. It sustains and energises the cosmos: the 'ground of all being'. It is the dynamic axis that generates all that has become, and is becoming. Although it has an 'essence of Being' that remains the 'same', this Energy enables all change to take place in creation: sometimes by evolution and mutation, sometimes through grace and miracles. It is available for all creatures, either for the continuation of life, or – as it manifests in the choices made by human beings – for the initiation of processes that may end in the destruction of our species and our world.

For me God is deeply mysterious: an Energy I cannot explain, but that exists at the heart of creation. What I do know is that I have deliberately committed myself to find this sustaining, continuous flow of Energy that I call Creative Love within nature, within the cosmos as we know it, and within the ordinary processes and rhythms of life and death. I am talking about a mystery that cannot be understood by reason alone, but whose presence in my life I continue to experience with joy.

The nearest I can get to making sense of my belief in this Energy-that-is-God is found in the opening chapter of St John's Gospel (Jn 1:1-18) and its description of cosmic Energy revealed – incarnated – in the person of Jesus. He is the only person who fully exhibits Unconditional Love in His life, through His death and resurrection, and through the abiding mysterious presence of the Holy Spirit. The presence of Unconditional Love in Jesus inspires me to follow him as closely as I can, even though I know that I fail to exhibit His degree of Love shown by the way He lived and taught.

My faith in the existence of Creative Love does not rely on the Bible alone, on creedal formulae, or upon a belief in Christ's miraculous conception. (To my mind the Energy of Love flowing into a woman through a natural conception is as great a miracle as any 'immaculate conception'.) Nor do I require Christ to lack the 'shadow side' of human nature. For when Christ is presented to me as 'tempted, yet without sin', he is too inhuman for me to try to follow. But when I see him embracing anger and remonstrating with the market sellers in the temple (Jn 2:13-22) or cursing a fig tree (Mk. 11:12-26), I can empathise with his humanity. And he shows me how I can protest – but still love those with whom I am angry.

This idea has become very important to me in that it raises awkward questions about how much of what we call sin is simply the result of the human condition and how much is deliberately chosen disobedience to God's will? While we are alive none of us, not even Christ, can escape the consequences of our animal nature: like Him we can sometimes express our humanity in thoughtless action against our parents as Jesus did when he stayed behind in the temple while his parents journeyed home (Lk 2:41-51), or when he ignored his mother when he was busy with his preaching work (Mt.12:46-50). It seems to me that in considering Jesus' sinlessness, we need to be clear that he was fully human, as well as fully divine. But much of what we confess as sin is not deliberate sin against God. It is the consequence of being human, and we should distinguish between these kinds of human errors and the deliberate sin that makes us turn our back on God. In that second sense, I do not consider Jesus did sin against the will of His Father at any time. He and the Father were One. Our devotional confessions do not separate us from God. Deliberate grave sins, deliberately chosen with full knowledge of what we are doing, do separate us from God, even though God never severs the bond of Love with us, but waits for us to repent. In that sense Jesus, is sinless in a way that no human being can be.

So can I call Christ God? Yes, because I do believe that God, the incarnate Jesus, the One who took flesh and emptied Himself into creation was truly one of us, yet remained deeply connected to the Energy behind all creation. Can I call Christ the embodiment of Unconditional Love? Yes. Can I believe that there is a connection between Unconditional Love and the creative Energy I have found in creation? Yes. Because for me, the pre-existent cosmic Christ, the second Person of the Trinity is, with the Creator and the Holy Spirit, the Source and Sustainer of all creation.

I continue to go to church because I need to: being too weak without the help of others to follow the Gospel imperatives that have guided my life for so long and have helped me to live a full and satisfying human life, even though I often betray them. I continue to go to church because the symbols used in the liturgy and worship point towards the reality both of God's transcendence and imminence. The 'real presence' of Christ in the Eucharist helps me to recognise that same Presence echoed in creation. Christ's willingness to enter my flesh and to 'abide in me' affirms His continued influence on my life and reveals to me the Creative Energy of Love at work all the time in created nature. I go because, even if each of the official doctrines of the Church were proved to have been untrue, I would still be a believer in that Unconditional Love and in its continuing outflow of creative energy in our time-bound creation.

Even beyond death

I have left to the last the greatest question of all: namely what happens after death? Each of us has to ask this question for ourselves. I have no firm answers. But I am willing to go on exploring because at this stage of my life I am concerned with the dynamic energy of love and the *goodness* of death.

I meet death each day. I know death's power in creation. I think, I explore, I hope, and I tremble before the cruel deaths that happen to people every day. Yet I continue to trust in the Creative Energy at work in creation. I want to learn how that Energy works to enable change within the span of a human lifetime. And I want to see which factors make it possible for human beings to co-operate with the Creative Energy to sustain life itself.

Some occasions of ecstasy and agony give us foretastes of physical death. Individuals, who find themselves in these situations realise that there is no possibility of return to any aspect of their former way of life. They have had a foretaste of the reality and permanency of death. They literally have to begin again: to be 'reborn' in some sense.

In this account of my journey from orthodox faith, through profound darkness and into a new way of living in the present moment, I know that I am taking a substantial risk of being totally misunderstood. I have not found it at all easy to discard prior knowledge so as to discover the experience of knowing that Unconditional Creative Love exemplified by the one person whose eternal Presence within the finite cosmos is the only criterion for my faith. All I can say in response to those who criticise my 'unorthodoxy' is that I have met Creative Love and I know it has changed my life. It has made it possible for me to believe in the goodness of the life-death-cycle of creation and to follow Jesus' creative teaching of love. I call Him Lord and so He is.

Chapter 8

Finding New Ways of Living

This chapter is the late fruit of my journeys with 'companions on the way': people I have met personally, but also my widespread encounters with nature and with the work of writers, artists, musicians and media communicators I may never meet. I am attempting to help people who are 'on the move' in their lives and also those who may accompany people who are crossing a bridge from one mode of life to another.

During the past twenty years or so I have encountered many people who have come to a heartbreaking event in their lives. And I have attempted to describe the stories of people who have had to reshape their lifestyles after such catastrophic incidents, to show that transformation can happen to many people. All of these encounters have enriched my life, even those involving cruelty, violence, sadism and masochism. At such times, caring for individual people is not enough: for we belong to communities, societies and nations. Consequently my own work has developed into a concern for the wider issues that affect the lives of the people I have encountered during a long and varied life. My own life journey has caused me to change in many ways and I expect I will continue to do so.

But before I get to the end of my mortal life I would like to share, in a practical way, some ideas about how ordinary people can help to improve the well-being of individuals and communities in today's world, to dream a few dreams and finally to tackle the thorny question as to how all that I have learnt through my own experience could contribute to the thorny question of the purpose of physical death.

In the preceding chapters I have tried to be honest about the apparent loss of my own religious faith, the manner of its transformation by a long battle with doubt, and the consequent death of some of the beliefs I once accepted. I have also outlined some of the crippling effects of coming to a 'full stop' through bereavement, the loss of hope, love, and trust in people and institutions. But, whether they happen to people of faith or to atheists, the question remains as to *what happens after such full stops?*

The blows I have described have been severe, certainly severe enough to deliver an initial 'knock out' blow to those who have undergone such ordeals. And, indeed, when a person comes to such a 'full stop' in his or her life it often *feels* terminal. Yet the impulse for recovery is so strong in most human beings that the majority of people in these situations do survive; in fact some of them do a great deal more than just survive. They may recover partially or fully able to continue the life they enjoyed beforehand. They may also find themselves transformed into a new way of living that amounts to a new birth.

For many years now I have been searching for the factors that help a person to survive in the first place and then to make the changes of direction that can subsequently lead to recovery or, indeed, to new birth, new life and new ways of being. When I began this search I was convinced that people of religious faith had an advantage over people without religious belief; and I suppose that I set out to prove that to myself. I have to say that is not my position now: I no longer need to contrive a role for religion in human survival strategies.

In the people I have met, of all religions and none, there is an innate drive towards survival and for life: if not for oneself, then certainly on account of children and grandchildren. This drive can, of course, be destroyed and towards the end of a long life it wanes. I now realise that I was somewhat arrogant in my youthful religious fervour to think that people of religious faith had an advantage over agnostics and atheists. It's just that those who do have religious faith, understand the urge to choose life as coming from God while, for those who have no need of God, it is simply the product of evolutionary development.

I have now spent some years of my retirement with people whom I have been privileged to know quite intimately, simply because they have trusted me with their innermost struggles for survival after they have come to a 'full stop', a turning point, in their life. And there is a pattern in their efforts that seems to me to be important to share with others who may be going through the same sort of struggles – although, of course, everyone's struggle is unique.

Caring for survivors

When a person arrives at the bottom of what feels like a fall into a deep dark crevasse she is stunned by the fall. There seems no place to hold on to and no way out. She may think that all hope of survival is lost and feel the full terror of weakening strength and increasing helplessness. She may fear that death looms.

Extreme examples of human survival after catastrophic accidents, disasters and threats to survival are well documented (32). They amaze many who read or hear about them: for they may find it almost unimaginable that they themselves would be capable of such heroism in similar situations. Yet, until they do, no one knows how they will react were they to face such disasters. There is, however, a subtle but distinct difference between survival of an incident followed by a full or partial recovery and one in which any return to a former way of life is impossible even though life continues. But what is it exactly that enables people to recover and return to all or much of what they were able to do before the 'full stop' event happened?

Self-protection as a means of survival

In the immediate period after any severe loss there is a period of bewilderment and numbness. It seems important not to make decisions during this period for precipitate decisions can often lead in the wrong direction. Often, however, there is a plethora of advice, various suggestions are proposed, and the victim of the sudden 'full stop' may become very bewildered by conflicting advice from those who are very far from the particular situation. Such advice is not always helpful. People may plead for space, ask 'to be left alone' or metaphorically 'turn their face to the wall'; and it is often wise for carers to refrain from uttering consoling thoughts at this stage. A good strategy to use is to delay making choices, even in regard to well-meant advice. That is not to say that one refuses all help. Advice that might lead to hasty action is to be avoided, but only for as long as it is necessary to recover the ability to make logical and calculated decisions. A cry of 'leave me alone' does not necessarily mean that someone is asking to be left alone *permanently*, and it is important for carers to return after a suitable time to enquire if the person's needs have changed.

The fact is that those who are seriously damaged by negative 'full stops' of life are eventually going to have to *help themselves to want to live*. They are going to have to mobilise their survival instincts if they are to believe that there is any point in remaining alive long enough to want to make a 'fresh start'. This takes time, much more than perhaps feels comfortable to either the person in question or to their relatives, friends and carers.

Patience can lead to recovery

A second helping strategy is patience: even though this goes against much contemporary thinking that prefers to hasten recovery, and even though victims of disaster often feel guilty that they are taking so long to recover. This is where wise carers will refrain from haste, and from advocating their own ideas about the 'expected norms' of behaviour. For people are highly complex and sensitive, and what is achievable by some is not necessarily achievable by others. (Some senior executives in professional institutions have proposed 'norms' about the right time for recovery: these then tend to become used to limit economic, legal or professional engagement with helping agencies. In that event some people will become casualties of the system and end up more handicapped than they would have been had they been assessed as individuals with particular difficulties and speed of recovery.)

It is often difficult for carers to gauge when and how to encourage someone to move forward. Some victims of disaster become afraid of any move towards even partial recovery and these need to be helped through very small steps toward greater involvement in some habitual activities by undertaking parallel activities unrelated to their usual work or previous lifestyle. Carers often have to search to find these and many suggestions will be rejected. I remember a profoundly sick patient who only started to take any interest in recovery when she was put in touch with someone who was similarly affected. Each felt understood by the other: and together they made progress that no carer had previously imagined. Indeed, the cheerful encouragement of the carers made matters worse for a time, because they presented the ill person with far too much challenge.

Letting go of the past

A third strategy for recovery is to encourage people to find ways of letting go of the past. This is not primarily concerned with forgiveness, either of themselves or of others, for what has befallen them. Paradoxically it is perfectly possible not to forgive, even to seek compensation from someone who has caused a permanent injury, yet still benefit from being willing to come to terms with the 'full stop'.

Indeed, my personal experience has repeatedly shown me that rage and lack of forgiveness can be a spur towards autonomy after an accident, misfortune, or injustice. Anger is a wonderful source of positive energy and, in the short term, can be therapeutic. But carers should be careful to help people to use it positively as a means of recovery, for long-term bitterness and self-pity can produce a passive apathy and stagnation in growth and attract the wrong kind of protective care that diminishes a person's quality of life.

Readjustment

Social isolation can, of course, lead to spiritual isolation and apathy, often followed by invalidism and dependency. It requires much patience on all sides, combined with repeated suggestions of possible ways of accomplishing a healthy disconnection between past and present in order to readjust to a new situation. Carers will expect to find resistance at first, but then may become discouraged and stop trying to facilitate forward thinking. This is a mistake. Finding creative ways forward is something that no one can accurately predict, and people have to be encouraged to get into an environment where there are ample and diverse opportunities for all kinds of creative activity. Those who get stuck at this stage need much help. And, except for keeping hope alive, a carer can perhaps do little in the initial stages of shock and depression other than seek help by the introduction of 'new' blood. Workers at rehabilitation centres are experts in patience and persuasion and those who are apparently imprisoned in fear and bereft of hope may then, despite their disability, subsequently agree to 'give it a try'. Once an injured person can accept the reality of their new situation more help, encouragement and praise for small accomplishments is essential. This is not the time to relax and let someone 'get on with it'. This is when the reality of each small change and achievement needs to be carefully charted so that new ways of living within a different context can be seen to be happening.

This is also the point at which risks must be taken: both by the person involved and by their carers. But those who have invested time, energy and love in caring for someone sometimes want to go on caring even when the person is obviously rearing to go and so they hold back the recovery process. Professional help for both parties is then necessary if confidence and momentum is to be maintained at this stage of convalescence. As a medical professional I have often failed to discern moments when challenge might have achieved more than sympathy, simply because of my own need to continue to offer pastoral care. And this is precisely why external supervision is essential. Moreover, this additional expenditure of effort to encourage recovery is entirely justifiable given its likely impact on families and social networks when a person starts to want to live life to the full. It is a great gift to all of us when we discover so many people who do live life to the full, despite only partial recovery. It inspires confidence in human ability to survive, develop and grow through disaster. We don't need to look to public heroes to find these people. They are in our own neighbourhoods helping those of us fortunate enough not to have met with such reverses in fortune to stop grumbling about our problems and get on with trying to live our own lives. But there are some people, like Franklin earlier, who never recover. Some, like Ruth – 'cut in half when her husband died' – are not able to return to their former way of life and need to go through transformative change and be 'born again'.

My husband's death

In my own life this happened in a quite obvious way when my husband had his stroke, but did not die physically. Both of us realised that this stroke was for us a foretaste of his physical death. We began to live in what we instinctively called 'end time'. We did not know whether Leo had a day, a week, a month or years of life to live before his death, but we knew he had tasted his death and so had I. Our attitudes towards time and our life together were completely changed by this recognition. Before Leo's stroke we would argue as any married couple do. We would express frustration, anger against one another, even when that partner was not to blame for our emotional turmoil. Bitter words, followed by mutual forgiveness and reconciliation, were fairly common in our family. Our expectations that we had a future together meant that there was plenty of time ahead to dream, plan, accomplish and make peace with each other.

After Leo's stroke we were changed people. We learnt to enjoy each present moment of life to the full. If we wanted to celebrate we did so, irrespective as to whether or not there was an impending birthday, festival time or other occasion for a party. We both took great care not to say unkind words to one another because we knew that those unkind words might be the last we ever exchanged. This was not a studied effort of any kind but now both of us had an altered view of time.

I had been a rather anxious wife before his stroke and sometimes rather over-protective for selfish reasons of wanting not to be separated by death. But now we took all sorts of risks during those seven years of waiting for his death. We took them knowing the possible consequences would be his death in my absence: yet for both of us – he in increasing weakness, I in my increasing ability to learn to live independently – this was one of the happiest times of our life together. I would leave him to go to work in the morning, sometimes sitting in an arm chair, sometimes basking in sunshine in the garden with his beloved companion dog beside him and his cat curled up in his lap. Dear friends and helpers would look in during the day, yet when I was coming home I never knew what state he would be in. Sometimes he was reasonably well, though very breathless; sometimes I would find him on the floor, or even in the greenhouse that he loved so much. We had no guilt about the risks we were taking by mutual consent and the absence of guilt provided us with great happiness in those years.

Towards the end of his life there was a poignant event. One day, when I was about to give him his pain relief injection, he turned to me and said: "Have you come to kill me today?" That very morning I had been praying that his suffering should come to an end swiftly. It would have been so easy to increase the dose. "No", I replied, "this very moment I selfishly want to go on keeping you alive." He relaxed. So did I. We could trust one another to tell the truth and know that the truth would be accepted. A few days later he died.

That is our story. Other people might live their 'end times' very differently. The great change in both of us was that we believed we should set one another free to enjoy life to the full until the very moment of his death. And we did.

I did not recover in the sense of going back to my former way of living. I had learnt to live 'out of time' and I have continued to live in 'end time' in the long years that have followed Leo's death, although it took me a while to learn to live in the joy of each present moment each day. Now that I am old, and have had foretastes of my own death, I live with calculated risks that help me to feel fully alive.

Living on the other side of the bridge: Janet's story

My personal story is both one of survival by recovery and of a mysterious encounter with death that lead to new birth and thus to the experience of crossing a metaphorical bridge and learning to live on the other side. Janet's story also illustrates this process.

This true story is about the very difficult reality of infertility which happens to some people. It begins with the fact that people don't know for certain that they can conceive a child before they do. People have no control over the ability to conceive – despite often imagining otherwise – and so when infertility happens, it is either a surprise or the fulfilment of an unspoken dread in the minds of one or both partners.

Janet knew she wanted children when she married. She was thirty-seven years old. She had a successful teaching career behind her and was eager to start a new phase in her life. Six months later she was still barren: sensibly, she sought help. That was the beginning of a long drawn out process of medical and surgical investigations. Two years later, nothing was clear. Her husband, Bruce, was fertile. She had no physical impediment to conception. The prognosis was complex, because it was thought that she might have had a hormonal condition that interfered with implantation and caused early miscarriages. The doctors thought they might be able to help. Hope was still alive. She agreed to treatment. Six conceptions and six profound disappointments later, she came to the end of her hope. Aged forty-four she could have gone on insisting that she wanted to try again, but her age and its attendant risks, deterred her. She stopped treatment, although her hope did not vanish entirely: it only disappeared some years later when her menopause was complete.

Janet entered a period of great unhappiness and bitterness. She had not wanted this to happen and fought against it. She knew, however, that her apparent success at concealing her inner misery had left a gnawing legacy of resentment. Sometimes she would find herself making cutting remarks about friends who were engulfed in parental problems with their teenagers. Sometimes, having no children to eat up family income, she flaunted her relative wealth in the quality of her clothes. Once, only once, she was slightly drunk and said that she was glad that she had never had children. Later, when she realised what an untruth she had told, she buried her head in her pillow and wept halfway through the night. The next morning she accepted a career advance that put her firmly in a higher income bracket. Janet was on a collision course for a nervous breakdown: and it happened.

She had never dealt properly with her unfounded subconscious anger at herself for being unable to carry a living child. This time help came through a number of professional people who had considerable insight into the delayed effects of significant frustrations and mistaken ways of compensating for them. Janet's breakdown was so severe that she needed a period of hospitalisation, during which she came to a self-understanding she had previously hidden even from herself. It was then that she realised that she had been healed. And this involved a transformative change in her attitude towards herself. Once the resentment was gone, once she had accepted her childlessness, she became able to enjoy other people's children in a new way and she eventually returned to her work as a fulfilled and happy teacher.

The greater part of Janet's ability to change direction came through her realisation that the complete loss of hope over one situation did not necessarily mean that the whole of her life was meaningless and a failure. She found hope that made her life fruitful again in a new way, but she could not have found that hope had she not come to terms with the real loss of her hopes of having children, forgiven herself for her sterility and moved into a new kind of fecundity through her work.

Perhaps the most important way of building bridges with people who have come to a 'living death' followed by a recognisable 'new birth' comes from carers who are content to wait until the first flicker of a determination to claim a new beginning, a new way of life, appears in those for whom they care. It is true that such a moment may never come. It is also true that the desire to "choose life, not death (Deut 30:19-20)," can be strong, even in the apparent absence of external evidence.

I have outlined some of the marks that may tell carers that the person they are caring for may have been touched by an energy that can be transformative, an energy that is also 'the ground of all being'. There is a discernable change of attitude in such people, a renewed desire to accept the end of one mode of being and to embrace another. They cease to judge themselves or others in terms of moral value. They accept the concept of mystery in life and are prepared to take the risk of exploration.

All movements towards life, in the full sense of that word, begin somewhere. They begin with a choice. There are signs that many of us are choosing life rather than death, that some of us are aware of the goodness of death as a gateway to life, not in some remote future, but for this present moment.

Chapter 9

Dreaming Dreams for the Future

It is time for this old person to "dream dreams (Joe1:28-29)." Although it may be true that older people remember more about the remote past than their recent experiences, dreaming is something they do very well. They have time on their hands, time spent waiting for the gift of death, time to be spent in wondering about the future of those they have brought into the world, and about the distant future of the planet. Older people can leave prophetic words and actions for the young. They are people who, in their half-waking half-sleeping lives, can reflect on the hopes they wish to be carried into a future that they will not actively share with those who are young.

I want to explore the role dreams play in motivating human action and change. For we know that some people do dream dreams in very specific ways and use them to make specific choices that alter their lives in ways that may also have implications for others around them.

Dreams that motivate waking action

This motivational form of dreaming is the one that interests me in the context of the kind of events that transform some people's lives in ways they never before thought possible. The transformation that follows such experiences is a kind of 'new birth' that is a foretaste of 'resurrection life' but which *cannot* be full resurrection life while we are still alive. In order to focus on this sort of dreaming, however, I need to distinguish it from certain kinds of other dreaming that may produce *illusionary* motivation that obscures the kind of motivational dreaming that might have a realistic chance of being fulfilled.

People have often recorded their sleeping dreams and waking

hallucinatory visions and we know a great deal about how the brain works when dreaming. How it deals with deep-seated anxieties and fears or frustrated sexual desire through bringing them into partial consciousness in dreams. How during sleep, suppressed and repressed emotions are liberated from conscious control; and how dreams can surface briefly into consciousness and be remembered on waking. Such dreams do not always directly lead to action but can motivate human beings to contemplate change. A man may wake from his dream about someone he has recently met and find himself determined to marry her. A woman might dream of herself as a nun in an enclosed convent and try to put that into effect, only to find she is totally unsuited to such a vocation. It is these motivational aspects of dreaming that originally captured my attention and helped me to note the way in which ancient writers spoke about dreams as a mode of communication between humans and their gods.

Motivational dreams have played an important part throughout human history. In previous generations most people thought that dreams, visions and hallucinations were a sign of God's favour, or the devil's intervention. Since it was difficult to discern exactly where the dream came from, people judged the dream by the effect it had on a person's behaviour. The Bible is full of descriptions of how God communicated in this way and sometimes causing people to alter their behaviour in quite dramatic ways.

One example comes from the prophet Joel who dreams of a future prosperity for God's people once they have repented of their sins and returned to the ways of God:

> You shall eat in plenty and be satisfied,
> And praise the name of the Lord, your God,
> Who has dealt wondrously with you.
> And my people shall never again be put to shame.
> And it shall come to pass afterward,

That I will pour out my spirit on all flesh
Your sons and your daughters shall prophesy,
Your old men shall dream dreams,
And your young men shall see visions.
Even upon your menservants and maidservants
In those days I will pour out my spirit (Joel 2:26-29).

Another is where Joseph is forewarned in a dream about Herod's evil intentions towards newborn children whom he intends to kill. That dream motivates him to take Mary and Jesus to Egypt, away from Herod's jurisdiction, until Herod's death when Joseph is told in a further dream that it is safe for them to return (Mt:2:13-21).

Dreams that contain hope for the future of humankind often invite us to go beyond the realm of purely logical thought into the realm of core values and beliefs that motivate us into actions that can change the course of history. That is why such dreams are so compelling, even though what is now known about the working of the brain dispenses with the need to attribute dreams, visions, and hallucinations to divine intervention.

Remembering dreams

During sleep, memories of past events may surface as dreams. While these may reflect ecstasies of past experience, they are often related to unpleasant incidents that we may not wish to recall and have suppressed or repressed. They can also uncover subconscious conflicts when the desire to change direction may clash with a desire to remain static. Some people cannot recall their dreams even though they are later aware that they were dreaming. They may feel uneasy or elated, frightened or calmed, after dreaming, but they cannot recall the dream itself. Yet some dreams, especially the repetitive ones, can be remembered. Remembering such dreams can be a way of recovering some internal motivational impulses and so affect the way people behave in determining future goals.

For me the importance of dreams, sleeping and waking, is that they have motivated me to action, not least my pre-occupation with justice for women and for homosexuals. And working in this field has led me to a personal transformation of my attitudes towards those with whom I have profoundly disagreed but with whom I have found it possible to find a unity in Love that has not destroyed either of our integrities. But my humanitarian work overseas, both as a missionary and as a member of the World Council of Churches and the Christian Medical Commission highlights a third emphasis of my life: the future of humankind and justice towards our planet and our environment.

I am still dreaming about these three concerns and, although I know that I will not see the outcome of these dreams, they give me the reason for writing this book. At the end of my life I still want to see religious faith as a positive contribution to the survival of humanity, and the religious conflicts that are happening all over our world must not prevail against the need to develop a global sense of community. I want to see religious faith harnessed for peace and not for war. But I am not looking to the great or the powerful for change, for they are as oppressed by their wealth as the poor people whom they oppress. I am looking to the ordinary people to begin a campaign of resistance and I want to see that resistance begin now. This is not some foolish idealistic dream. Our ancestor's dreams have been fulfilled, if only in part, in regard to slavery and racism. And it can be done again. Prophets cannot be content to die without saying this. Gradually the message will spread, not today, nor tomorrow, nor next year, but it has to begin somewhere and it can begin with a few individuals who are willing to put their core beliefs and religious faith into action.

Justice for oppressed people

I started peace and justice work because my mother and I

suffered deprivation when I was a child. When I realised that my separated parents were not going to be reunited I turned my attention to the poverty that my mother and I suffered in consequence and becoming a medical student in the early days of the National Health Service taught me about the ills of suffering, classism, racism, and sexism.

When I 'dream dreams' for the future, my hope is for the gradual elimination of ignorance. I work towards, through argument, open witness and crossing all kinds of boundaries set up to exclude those of whom we are afraid because they are different. I cannot rest until justice comes for people whom God has created in love to be the persons they are. God wants women and men to live in ways that are free from external oppression. That is why I witness in my family, in my community, in my society and in the world. I can do no other. That is why I long for Christians throughout the world to change their attitudes towards those whom they oppress. This will not happen in a day. It is an evolutionary process and such Spirit-inspired conversion of manners will happen among many people: not just through a few who desire to bring about change by force. I do not decry the value of revolution under certain circumstances of oppressive injustice, but evolution and God-given grace-filled inspiration achieves more in the long run.

Sexism and gender discrimination

I have written about my experiences in Africa as a medical missionary. At that time I was unable to do very much to help the women I cared about. Later back home I was able to act, but I still did not appreciate the depth of institutional sexism that was prevalent in Churches and social institutions in the late 1960s and 1970s. The sexism was everywhere in all classes; but it was made worse in the Churches by the kind of single-sex, male-only private boarding school mentality whose patriarchal attitudes were visibly expressed in, or more often hidden under, benevolent paternalistic attitudes towards women. These attitudes were ingrained and I and some other Christians thought they needed addressing for the benefit of society.

We could not accomplish change on our own: so we found allies, particularly in Women in Media and other feminist movements (33). At the beginning of our work we realised that some of the theological objections to the ordained ministry of women and to the issue of the 'headship' of women over men were complex in nature and strongly affected by pre-modern beliefs about, for instance, the roles of men and women in conception; attitudes promoted in the Catholic Church. We knew it would be hard to change these views, but we also thought that the evolutionary processes involved in the education and development of women's skills were urgently needed in our own time. And many of us will continue to persist with our advocacy.

That is how I and others became involved in the life of the Church. We thought that women's voices and wisdom were, and are, needed in the decision-making processes and developments of the ministry of the Anglican Church. The Nonconformist Churches had made a start: we thought we should too. And I still believe that the Catholic and Orthodox Churches need women in their ordained ministries and decision-making processes. For the influence of all Churches on social justice issues is diminished by these continuing sexist practices. I can only hope that, in the future, people will wonder what the fuss was all about because it will be irrelevant to the survival of our planet and everyone will have to focus on more critical matters for life on earth to continue.

Looking back thankfully

Much of this book has been about my life and work among underprivileged, vulnerable and oppressed people as a medical doctor, cleric and 'soul friend' with women and with lesbian, gay, bisexual, transgendered and intersex people. All this work has been undergirded by my Christian faith about the nature of my womanhood and its effect of my public working life and Christian ministry.

In 1975, the year when the Sex Discrimination Act became law, I published *Flesh of my Flesh,* a book that was based on my hope that women and men would begin to "rediscover the joys of partnership with each other, the relief of being able to share decisions, the meaning of real community, [and] the purpose of whole living for their own and the common good (34)." I thought that the Church of England would be an ideal place to put this hope into action. After all, I then thought, it was concerned with the nature of human beings in relationship to their Creator and with the whole of creation. I expressed my hope by saying that I believed that there was "an urgent necessity, or women and men to make fresh beginnings in relationships by gathering together to reflect upon their common humanity, and to put into action their joint discoveries about relationship (35)."

I have now had nearly forty years to see what happened to my hopes when I wrote that book. No one can say that the initial dialogue about women's roles in the Church of England took place with a 'gathering together to reflect on their common humanity'. Dispute, conflict, dominion, confusion and endless arguments from polarised positions, resulted in the reluctant acceptance of women priests in 1993. Those pioneer women clergy found themselves living with discriminatory laws when the State approved the legislation and so allowed the Church to be exempt from the common law of the land. The polarisation and formation of groups with separate identities and demands for recognition worsened after the Act of Synod and its subsequent implementation – now twenty years ago – when women were first ordained.

I watched what happened to these women pioneers. Many of us had neither the training, nor the experience of the kind of responsibility that their male counterparts had been brought up with since childhood. Some of us, who had never worked outside the Church in jobs that carried considerable responsibility, found it hard to adjust our behaviour appropriately. Some of us, who had previously held jobs where authority had been natural to us found ourselves frustrated by the restrictions to our ministries: even to the point where we 'shook the dust off our feet and walked away'. Initially the women who came into the ordained ministry found themselves among a majority of male priests who had never before encountered women in their priestly profession. Inevitably both groups made mistakes and found ourselves in difficult situations, and though relationships between women and men have improved greatly in the twenty years that have followed, we still argue about the effect of our femaleness and our maleness on our roles in the Church of England.

Rediscovering mutuality

At this point in my life I realise that for a very long time I have felt – and do still feel – strongly about the goodness of being a woman. I believe that this demands that women be welcomed into every strata of society. Women and men need to be *partners together*, rather than role models for separate sexual functions. And I deeply regret all forms of discrimination, all prescriptive ideas about how each sex should think, react and behave, and all stereotyping of whatever kind.

Although I am a fertile woman, who has born and reared four children, I believe that the nature of all women confers on them the potential of motherhood. I believe too that the material fact of womanhood has a spiritual potential that is a vital component of society. God incorporates femaleness and maleness into creation and loves, and uses both equally according to their potential. (That parenthood may result in an experience of unity that predates birth, the relinquishment of control over personal contributions to the product of their union. This relinquishment of control is most obvious in the experience of conception where men relinquish their control of their destiny through a multitude of their sperm. In receiving sperms, a woman relinquishes control over their joint future. The miracle of birth brings them to a deeper understanding of their joint need to protect, nurture and develop the newborn child who is a distinct and separate human being. As a Christian I believe that this dependence on creative energy is mutual and is reflected in a spiritual dimension of human relationships. This spiritual dimension of partnership can also be accomplished in those who do not have children, those in same sex partnerships, those who have to endure bereavement from a beloved partner.)

My experience of being single, married and a widow, celibate since 1998, suggests that the potential for motherhood and fatherhood in all women and men can unite them in parenthood: for spiritual motherhood and spiritual fatherhood are both needed for the creative developments that will enable us to continue God's work on earth until the consummation of God's creative work.

Discovering our humanity

Since women were ordained into Non-conformist ministries and the historic ministries of the Anglican Churches, arguments have raged about whether or not they include distinctiveness of function or headship in any manner. I was a party to endless discussions of this sort both before women were ordained in the Anglican Church and since. So when women were ordained I was eager to watch the outcome. Does the womb matter? Will women bring a special 'nuance' to ministry? Is equality of function as deacons, priests and bishops necessary? Can the Church survive with a male-only ministry: or should we do away with men and just manage with women? Is there a difference between male language and female language, male ways of doing things and female ways of doing things?

The needs of this generation of people demand that we reconsider what it *means to be a human being* rather than a man or a woman. If we focus on our common humanity we might be able to recover a sense of community in society and amongst nations find new ways of being human beings in relationship with each other for the common good, and so anticipate the needs of future generations and of creation itself. It is, I think, when women and men work together in harmonious partnership that their humanity has the greatest potential for wholeness. That is why I felt that women should become priests. That is what motivated me and still motivates me. Spiritual motherhood and spiritual fatherhood are vital to the well-being of society and Churches and faith organisations alike. Theologically Christ assumed *human* flesh, not just male flesh: else women could not be redeemed.

All that I believed before women were ordained in the Anglican Church has been put to the test. It may be too early to judge the outcome. Indeed, I think it is. Yet I, more than most people, have had the opportunity to see both men and women in action within the priesthood within the past twenty years and I really cannot see what all the fuss is about so long as we remember that women and men are equal human beings, and precious individuals created by the energy of Love for life in all its fullness.

I testify to my delight when I see women and men working together, when I see women at the altar and men at the altar, when I shake hands with a female bishop and with a male bishop: providing that each behaves in a human way, rather than demanding submission and subordination. I believe that Christian women ministers, pastors, deacons, priests and bishops are needed in all our communities. I believe that they will bring blessing to society and countries where women have no educational or social rights, or scanty rights. I am thankful to have had a small share in bringing about the ordination of women in the Anglican Churches in Britain and to have worked so closely with women in other Churches to achieve the changes in attitude that have come about.

I rejoice and rejoice again that the Anglican Church that I love has had the courage to ordain women. I continue to long for the day when that love and respect is extended to other Anglican communions and nations where women are thought of in stereotypical ways and confined to domesticity. And now, as a Catholic I do not want to leave pastoral work to celibates, be they nuns or priests. We need the insights and experience of married people in priestly and pastoral work.

One day we will learn how it is that Creative energy wants us to be. The time will come and each small step towards that day will prepare the way towards peace and harmony in the world. I shall not see it, but someone will. I see the future from a historical perspective on the development of human rights and responsibilities. We are a species that is still evolving and my hope and my prayer in my old age is that the evolutionary processes of natural selection and Spirit-led inspiration will ultimately achieve a more human and humane society, a more equable and peaceful co-existence for all in our world. I hope with all my heart that those who live after me will continue that process. Indeed one of the signs that such work is continuing has come from two brave young women. One of them, Malama Yousafi, has challenged the oppression of women in those countries that have governments that discriminate against women. The other, Fahma Mohamed, is actively campaigning against female genital mutilation. I give thanks that I have seen and heard these two young women before I die.

Justice for the earth

It is not our vocation as human beings to look towards the end of time, to hasten it through destructive means, to destroy creative energy wantonly, and to put the value of our own lives above those of future generations who will have to live with the consequences of our decisions and actions. My involvement in environmental protection issues began in 1962 when I read Rachel Carson's *Silent Spring* (36). At this time there were relatively few voices expressing concern about the serious effect of human activities on the environment of the planet on which we depend.

I was also influenced by Barbara Ward, later Baroness Jackson of Lordsworth, who was an advisor to policymakers in Britain and the United States of America. With René Dubois she published *Only One Earth: The Care and Maintenance of a Small Planet* for the 1972 UN Stockholm Conference on the Human Environment that saw the establishment of the United Nations Environmental Project (37). I became even more active in 1974 when I heard of the protest of Chipko women who hugged trees to protect them from loggers in Chamoli in the Indian Himalayas, an issue brought to the attention of the world by Vendana Shiva, an Indian physicist and environmentalist campaigner at the Mexico City Conference of 1975 (38). I continue to read widely, support environmentalist protectors and international figures like Al Gore and Maathai Wangari (39) through prayer and signing petitions. I shall continue to pray and support those who are younger than I in their work.

Since then millions of people have become aware of the current changes in our natural environment, many of which are decidedly related to human activities. Warnings have been issued by a multitude of international bodies and gatherings. Though some of their suggestions have been resisted by powerful international and multinational bodies, some progress towards global awareness of the situation has been made, yet relatively little has been achieved by global consensus. Now the lives of millions of human beings are adversely affected, and the current state of our planet seems to be under threat.

Ordinary people can have much more influence than they think. While some feel helpless in the face of continuing destructive human activities and simply despair. Others, including myself, believe that we need to continue to advocate changes in human attitudes. We can resist oppression. We can stop buying goods that diminish the life expectations of the producers. We can buy fairly-traded goods, support ethical companies, and resist the mechanisation of life. We can develop increased respect for the lives of all created beings and refuse to support corruption. We can refuse to go to war. Peace and justice *are* achievable, but they *will* not come through powerful people, but rather through the actions of many, as Green Peace members are showing (40).

Yet words without actions are not going to be an effective witness. That is why I offer some suggestions about practical action in our current environmental situation.

Time for Action

Our actions have to be motivated by the thought of our great-grandchildren who will suffer because of our present complacency.

- We can assume responsibility for how we use even the little money we have to support peace and justice throughout the world.

- We can withdraw money and support from groups of people or institutions that are misusing our trust.

- We are able to protest. Our protest can take the form of civil disobedience. But if we take that path we must expect substantial personal and corporate suffering.

Our actions will be costly.

- We can control the money we have available for spending or investing. We can decide to limit our spending on extravagances and decide to live more simply in order to support others.

- We can employ more people at a decent wage and refuse to buy goods from those who exploit the poor.

Witness matters.

- We have to find the courage of our convictions and banish the thought that 'nothing will ever change'. We must begin to believe that our views matter. Without witness we cannot help others to effect similar changes in their lives.

We can gather hope and strength from one another as we begin to make an impact. Our governments and multinational corporations may change only when they lose our support, only when we deprive them of money on which to feed their greed.

You can make a difference

One individual's sense of personal responsibility for the future of our species and our planet can change the world. I do not need a Pope, a bishop, a president, a prime minister to tell me that. I have to do it myself. Change is possible. Faith does move mountains.

Changes start to happen when one person dreams a dream and is motivated towards action. Such changes gather strength as others catch the vision. Dreams for the future well-being of our species, our planet, and even the cosmos, can effect change when a large number of ordinary people add their voices to the debate. Change of direction is always hard on individuals and resistance will be inevitable, though it will only become violent if those who hold power are violently suppressive of the hopes of the many. Yes, sometimes those people who want to bring about change will suffer grievously and may even have to pay with their lives.

But sometimes death can be the one and only event that provokes change and transformation. It falls to us to act if we wish to avoid the reality of our great-grandchildren locked into violent confrontation to find water, food and shelter in a barren world, It is, in short, up to the ordinary citizens of the world to rebel, protest, use whatever collective people-power we can muster to bring about the revolutionary change the world now needs.

Former Anglican Archbishop Desmond Tutu famously said "I am a prisoner of hope (41)." When I heard him say that I joined him. And when I say this, then I know my hope cannot be in vain. It will bear fruit in my life, old and near to death though I am.

This fruit ripens when I take personal responsibility for my own actions that support the exploitation and impoverishment of others. When I amend my life, and become willing to live with less so that others might live at all. When I amend the ways I use money in order to give proper worth to those I continue to oppress. When I amend the trust I put in large institutions so that they can change. When I amend my selfishness and need for material comfort, in order to preserve a good quality of life for future generations. And when I amend my willingness to witness to this and to suffer for it. But if I do this, if I dream dreams and amend my ways, I know that I will be joining others who, down the centuries, have felt and acted in much the same way.

What I am saying is nothing new. For my dream comes from a deep faith in the witness and teachings of Christ that is part of my natural inheritance, my own upbringing and culture, and my own vocation: the long working out of which has made me a prisoner of hope for the future, a believer in the prompting of dreams and a woman who has dared act towards their fulfilment.

Acknowledgements

This book is the fruit of many years struggle to clarify my thinking and beliefs. I am indebted to my bishop guardian The Rt Rev Dominic Walker OGS; my former spiritual director the late Fr Donald Allchin; and all the Catholic and Anglican members of religious orders who have listened to me, shared their thoughts with me and encouraged me to continue to engage in exploration throughout their spiritual care for me. I learned a great deal from the vicars and chaplains with whom I have worked, especially the Revds Donald Reeves, Frances Cumberledge, Len Crowe, James Coutts, Keith Denerley and Ian Stamp. I am indebted to Ms Sue Dowell, a member of the Christian Parity Group, who stood with me when I shouted at General Synod in 1978 and to all our supporters in our years of struggle.

I am grateful to the Revd Dr Terry Biddington, the Revd Elaine Dando, Dr Jill Robson PhD, and Hugo Perks for robust comments on early texts and especially to Terry Biddington for technical help with the production of this book. I also wish to thank the many people who have allowed me to share something of their journeys over a period of many decades.

All Biblical quotations are taken from the New Standard Version, Oxford University Press, New York, 1989.

Notes

1   Frederick Temple, Archbishop of Canterbury (1896-1902).

2   George Alexander Hill, *Go Spy the Land*, Cassell, London, 1932 and *Dreaded Hour*, Cassell, London, 1936 are books in which he wrote about his espionage activities in the First World War.

3   Donald Nicholl, Catholic theologian, author of *Holiness*, DLT, London, 1981 and many other books.

4   The National Health Service was established in July 5th 1948. So I began life as a hospital medical student a year before its inception and saw its inauguration during my student days and internships.

5   D.C.W. Northfield, Surgeon in charge of Neurosurgical department at London Hospital 1938-1967. Died: 18.07.1986.

6   Denis March, SSF, Vicar of St Benet's. He was my spiritual director for many years.

7   Community of the Holy Name founded in 1865 in Vauxhall London to help poor and deprived people in that area by Fr William Herbert and Mother Francis Mary. The Community moved to Malvern Link, Worcestershire in 1887 and then to Derby in 1984.

8   Order of the Holy Cross founded in 1884 by Fr James Otis Sargent Huntingdon in 1884 in New York City under an Augustinian Rule. Now a Benedictine order near the Hudson River in New York State.

9   Donald Reeves, M.B.E, Parish priest of St Helier, Founder and Director of The Soul of Europe for Peace building in the Balkans.

10. Mary Stott (1907-2002). The longest serving editor of the Guardian newspaper's Women's Page from 1957-72. She was opposed to discrimination in all its forms and encouraged younger women to take their own initiatives. I met her on

the Hyde Park march and she and the Women in Media group gave me support in my campaigning work.

11 When I was first made a deaconess this was true. Women Readers were allowed to preach at Holy Communion and the anomaly was quickly put right.

12. Rev Florence Li Tim-Oi (1907-1992). She was ordained priest in 1944 in Hong Kong in response to a crisis among Chinese Christians due to the Japanese invasion. Her ordination was controversial when it became known after the end of World War Two and she resigned her licence but always maintained her priesthood. She eventually moved to Canada during her retirement.

13 Rev Joyce Bennet OBE 1923-. Ordained by Bishop Hall in 1974 with Jane Hwang. Her Orders were not accepted when she retired to England in 1982. She was appointed to St Martin in the Fields, London to care for a Chinese speaking congregation.

14 Gustavo Gutierrez, *A Theology of Liberation*, Orbis Books 1988, SCM, England.

15 South Bank Theology was propounded at an ecumenical conference between Anglicans and Catholics in 1966. http://archive.catholicherald.co.uk/article/22.July-1966/8/mixed-clergy-debate-south-bank-theology.

16 Una Kroll, *TM- a Signpost for the World*, D.L.T, London, 1974.

17 The stories of organisations and individuals are told in Margaret Webster, *A New Strength, A New Song*, Mowbray/Cassell 1994.

18 Christian Medical Commission founded by World Council of Churches to promote the coordination of national church related medical programmes and to engage in study and research into the most appropriate ways in which the churches might express their concern for total health care.

19. The Society of the Sacred Cross, a contemplative religious order of Anglican women in Monmouth.

20 Women in the Church in Wales were only ordained in January1997, three years later than their sisters in England because of an adverse vote in the Welsh Synod in 1993.

21 Terry Waite, *Taken on Trust*, Hodder & Stoughton, London, 1994.

22 The Christian absolutist view of marriage is that a sacramental marriage before God is indissoluble except by death. If a marriage is dissolved by secular law it is not dissolved by God, and so the separated partners cannot validly remarry sacramentally until the former partner is dead.

23 Many Christian Churches have modified their attitudes to remarriage after divorce, but wide differences in individual practice continue to confuse people in particular situations.

24 The International Commission on English in the Liturgy was set up for the purpose of providing English translations of the liturgical books of the Roman Rite. www.wikipedia.org/ICEL accessed 24/03/14.

25 This is a technical term that is sometimes used to describe a relationship between two people on a spiritual journey towards union with God. It is not a directive relationship in which obedience to the director plays a part, but one in which two people keep company on a journey that both of them are undertaking.

26 1998 Lambeth Conference Resolution on Human Sexuality 1:10 4 states that "while rejecting homosexual practice as incompatible with Scripture, calls on all other people to minister pastorally and sensitively to all irrespective of sexual orientation and to condemn irrational fear of homosexuals." Resolution 1.10.5 states that LC "cannot advise the legitimising or blessing of same sex unions, nor ordaining those involved in same gender unions and we wish to assure them that they are loved by God, and that all baptised, believing and faithful persons, regardless of sexual orientation are full members of the Body of Christ."

27 Lambeth 2008 reaffirmed these resolutions and made no further decisions but recommended that listening to homosexual persons should continue and a Covenant be set up to ensure compliance within the 1988 framework. This is still in process. Meantime a separate dissenting body, GAFCON, has been set up as an alternative structure by those who reject active homosexual practice, blessing of civil partnerships and gay marriage by Christians, that is now (2014) legal by State laws in some Anglican Provinces, and illegal and subject to imprisonment and active persecution in others. The Anglican Communion remains in serious internal conflict about these issues.

28. Gene Robinson, was consecrated as a bishop of the Protestant Episcopal Church of the United States of America on 04.08.2003. His consecration precipitated the serious conflict that remains unresolved.

29 William James, *Varieties of Religious Experience* 1902, Longman's Green & Co. Margarita Laski, & Antony Bloom, *Living Prayer,* 1st edn.1993. This contained a conversation between Bloom (an Orthodox priest) and Laski (a Jewish atheist) that was very influential on my thinking at the time I was a theology student.

30 Paul Tillich (1886-1965) said that God, the "Ground of Being," is separate from the finite realm and that anything brought from essence into existence is always going to be corrupted by ambiguity and finitude. He questioned whether or not there was a God above God i.e. a God above God in the Incarnate Jesus. See his *Systematic Theology,* Vol 1. His theories have not been generally accepted.

31 I value Darwin's *Origin of Species* and know about some of the anomalies in the theory. I accept the general principles of the theory but am not a strict Darwinian of the 'Dawkin's school'. The word 'grace' is used here in a theological sense, namely that it is spiritual help given by God to rational

beings as a means of their sanctification.

32 Joe Simpson, *Touching the Void*, Vintage, Random House, London 2004.

33 "Women in Media" was founded in the 1970s by a group of women working in the media who felt they were discriminated against in pay and opportunity by institutional sexism in their industry belonged to this group.

34 Una Kroll *Flesh of My Flesh*, DLT, London, 1975, p.106.

35 Ibid p.106.

36 Rachel Carson, *The Silent Spring*, Houghton Mifflin USA. 1962.

37 Barbara Ward Jackson, Rene Dubois, Maurice F Strong, *Only One Earth*, Routledge, London, 1983.

38 See htp://www.huffingtonpost.com/Biancajagger/women the=unsung=heroes-o_b_2838414. Accessed 26.8.2013.

39 Wangari Maathai, en.wilkipedia.org/wiki/Wangari Maathai

40 The Green Peace Movement evolved from the Peace Movement and anti-nuclear protests of the 1960s and 1970s.

41 Desmond Tutu, on BBC News *Breakfast with Frost*, on 29.05. 2005.

Appendix:

List of Publications by Una Kroll

TM-A Signpost for the World, London: DLT, 1974
Flesh of My Flesh, London: DLT, 1975
Lament for a Lost Enemy, London: SPCK, 1977
Sexual Counselling, London: SPCK, 1979
The Spiritual Exercise Book, London: Firethorn Press, 1985
Growing Older, London: Collins, 1988
In Touch with Healing, London: BBC Books, 1991
Vocation to Resistance, London: DLT, 1995
Trees of Life, London: Mowbray, 1997
Crossing the Boundaries, Norwich: Canterbury Press, 1999
Forgive and Live, London: Mowbray, 2000
Anatomy of Survival, London: Mowbray, 2001
Living Life to the Full, London: Continuum, 2006

CHRISTIAN
ALTERNATIVE

Throughout the two thousand years of Christian tradition there have been, and still are, groups and individuals that exist in the margins and upon the edge of faith. But in Christianity's contrapuntal history it has often been these outcasts and pioneers that have forged contemporary orthodoxy out of former radicalism as belief evolves to engage with and encompass the ever-changing social and scientific realities. Real faith lies not in the comfortable certainties of the Orthodox, but somewhere in a half-glimpsed hinterland on the dirt track to Emmaus, where the Death of God meets the Resurrection, where the supernatural Christ meets the historical Jesus, and where the revolution liberates both the oppressed and the oppressors.

Welcome to Christian Alternative... a space at the edge where the light shines through.